I love how Dr. Low's book opens the door to a world of
spiritual philosophies and practices which provides the reader
an opportunity for self discernment… whether you are on the
very first step of your spiritual awakening or have been on your
path for years, this book has something to offer you!

Rev. Carolyn Stern, Interfaith Minister & Licensed Massage Therapist

David's book is an incredible testament to his life's work on his
own spiritual path. Not only does he include many of the psycho-
spiritual traditions, but also the body/mind issues…so it is truly
a new kind of comprehensive spiritual textbook to be studied
and pondered over. This is a man who has lived the spiritual path
for many, many years, and now can become one its best teachers
because of his understanding and personal experiences.

*Carol Day, Pathwork Helper, Craniosacral/Energy therapist,
and former faculty, Barbara Brennan School of Healing*

David Low's book offers a haven of basic understanding
of spiritual concepts and terms, and also clarifies some
misunderstandings. It is simple in the best sense of the word,
because its intent is to avoid the sometimes disorienting content
of spiritual books: too complex, too dogmatic, too "woo woo"
etcetera… it frees seekers from such burdens, so they can be more
sure-footed on the path they choose or are already walking.

Paco Tozan Vérin, Priest, Hollow Bones Zen Order

In affectionate memory of

Baruch Spinoza
(1632–1677)

Who forged the first true union of science and spirit

Universal Spiritual Philosophy and Practice

An Informal Textbook for
Discerning Seekers

David Low, MS, PhD

Illustrated by Juliet Montefusco

Contents

PART 2   PHILOSOPHICAL UNDERSTANDINGS

PART 3   THE MECHANICS OF SPIRITUALITY

Hatred that is fully overcome by love passes into love, and the love will therefore be greater than if it had not been preceded by hatred.

BARUCH SPINOZA

ETHICS III, P.44

Introduction

Why You Might Like this Book

Universal Spiritual Philosophy and Practice is meant for anyone who is searching, or otherwise disillusioned with where the spiritual journey has taken him or her. It aims to be a systematic, practical exposition of important mystical understandings which all religions share. For the sake of brevity, it largely excludes less radical points of view.

My main assumption is that there are many common dimensions and experiences between different people's spiritualties—which hold whether those experiences occur within, between, or outside of the religions, whether the seeker is educated or religious or not, and regardless of cultural background.[1] I also think there are common ways in which basic spiritual principles are not understood, which frequently hold people back.

The concept of enlightenment is of particular concern. In order to discuss it objectively, it is necessary to assume that enlightenment is, as some scholars say, *normative*—representing the same quality across all traditions and personalities. But the human organism varies in its capacities, and it may be that the enlightened state is more effectively channeled through some more than others. That said, there is a strong consensus from the great teachers that self-realization is the same for everyone who experiences it. The second thing to mention up front is that, although enlightenment is not always associated with spiritual seeking as we usually understand it, for systematic understanding we must generally assume that it is. If the exceptions mentioned here are confusing, no apologies are offered—it comes with the territory.

> *My main assumption is that there are common dimensions between different people's spiritualties–whatever their culture or background.*

The material is dense in places and hopefully the pictures and graphics will facilitate reading. The luminaries are meant to provide a more easygoing, kind of parallel learning experience, and the off-sets echo or supplement the material in hopefully interesting ways. For the most part I have intentionally avoided examples and detailed explanations; what I hope some will find unique is the pithy way that mystical truths are delineated and given relevant, perhaps entertaining contexts. Naturally however, in trying to cover so many aspects of a topic this profound, I am sure that my own biases intervene here and there. Ultimately, we only take from a book what we find valuable, and leave aside the rest.

Many concepts employed here have long since entered the popular vocabulary and no longer need much citing or explanation. Although I do assume some familiarity with philosophical and spiritual references, most of the points I make can be understood without them. Some observations draw upon or summarize entire fields pertinent in some way to spirituality, which readers can investigate on their own. For these reasons, footnotes often refer simply to important writers or entire books in different areas.

As in other textbooks, I write as an authority, and therefore make very few "I-statements" (I think… My experience has been… etc.). I mention this because this kind of material is rarely set down in an impartial way. This book is basically a blend of widely accepted observations in philosophy and psychology with what would normally be considered subjective testimony from a great many peoples' similar experiences. Because there has always been a wide consensus among accomplished mystical seekers that a certain view does represent ultimate truth, this view—monism or essentialism—is strongly favored over other views in this book, and constitutes its "bias."

While I haven't done the research necessary to substantiate all my observations, I'm sure that most everything within the academic realm that I mention has already more or less been expressed in a reputable journal or book somewhere. My apologies to anyone I don't acknowledge.

Due to the nature of the material, many chapters and sections are self-contained. For the most part, readers can jump ahead without reading the material that preceded it. The chapter and section references scattered throughout—inspired by how Spinoza wrote his *Ethics*—allow you double-check and reread sections for better understanding.

D.L.
September, 2015
david@worldspirituality.com

KWAN YIN ON DRAGON— *Chinese Buddhist and Taoist deity. Superficial meaning: The patroness of fishermen in the South China Sea flying over ocean. Profound meaning: Inner, purifying spiritual energy guided by God (Self), as well as primal urges mastered by the same.*

PART 1

PRELIMINARIES

The first part of a new spiritual initiative, whether undertaken consciously or not, involves the willingness to rethink basic attitudes and assumptions. Everyone *has* a spirituality, however discouraged we may be about getting in touch with or finding more of it. (I remember reading of one person who spoke of himself, saying, "I don't think engineers can have a spiritual experience.")

We often don't recognize that although they may not have *developed* in the same way and to the same extent, **everyone** possesses the same psycho-spiritual faculties at the different levels of their being. This goes for believer, agnostic, atheist, the mentally challenged (wiring can be underdeveloped) *and* the criminally insane (things can get out of balance).

DOVE OF THE HOLY SPIRIT—
*Christian Symbol. Superficial meaning:
the Holy Spirit descending, in the form of
a bird, upon Jesus at his baptism. Profound
meaning: Energy of God/Self (grace)
granting some level of spiritual illumination
or full enlightenment, either temporarily
or permanently, to any seeker ready for it.
Courtesy Wikimedia Commons.*

CHAPTER ONE

Beliefs, Attitudes, and Experiences In Spirituality

There are some elementary things people often have misconceptions about, which need to be cleared up before we proceed. They have to do with what spirituality is, how it is experienced, and its relationship to modern science, especially physics and psychology. For many, this scientific connection imparts to spirituality a relevance and plausibility it didn't used to have.

1 Spirituality and "Experiences"

Spirituality is defined here as the part of religion that all religions have in common. As such, it is fundamentally mystical, transcending all cultures, languages, histories, and even personalities. It seems to involve our personalities, because we each interact with the great mystery (God/ Self) in our own unique way, even though it's the same great mystery.

First we need to put to rest a basic misconception about "spiritual experiences." It is sometimes thought that finding your spirituality is always about having some definite inner experience that tells you that you're doing the right thing—some momentary bliss or interior *wow!* confirmation that you're on the right path.

Put this idea out of your head.

First, it's great if you have such experiences, but for most people it's more often about faith: the simple conviction that the things you are doing are helping your spirituality, maybe if only little by little, and that there is a gradual and slow transformation going on of a permanent, lasting nature inside you, way beneath the radar. You are not, after all, interested in some buoyant mood or illusory phase of happiness that won't last. As time goes on and you do your work, this "faith" will slowly grow into a deep and profound joy.

> *The inherent average mood you experience—THAT'S your spirituality, right now!*

In a sense, belief is experience. The inherent average "mood" a person experiences, be it joyful, depressed or whatever, is what he or she believes 100%, without reservation. That *itself* is the person's experience of God or divinity. It's "where you're at"—as God as created you, right now.

The reason a lot of people don't get into spiritual paths is because they don't experience anything as "missing" from their lives—at least, according to their current understanding of what life is, or what it is possible for life to offer them.

2 Psychological And Spiritual Growth The Same

Another natural tendency some of us have is to separate psychological growth from spiritual growth, since we usually go to different places and get different methodologies for each. But ultimately they are the same. A good spirituality assumes good mental health, and cannot develop in the most balanced way without it. Although it can involve opposing qualities ("toughlove" verses sympathy) spirituality is about self-knowledge, which increases as we develop greater appropriate love, compassion, tolerance, and sacrifice for ourselves and others. Alleviating depression, getting along better with your spouse, overcoming addiction, discovering your aptitudes—anything constructive that you might approach some kind of psychologist for helps your spirituality. It was Jung who said that every patient over 35 whom he dealt with experienced problems which ultimately stemmed from a lack of connection to a deeper, spiritual sense of meaning.[1] It's

> *Practically speaking, spirituality and mental health can be more or less EQUATED.*

definitely helpful, therefore, for some people to engage more in the psychological/therapeutic aspect of personal growth, instead of the spiritual aspect of that growth. (It will be necessary for me to occasionally step into a psychological frame of reference to remind us

Some are better off engaging the PSYCHOLOGICAL rather than the "spiritual" aspect of spiritual growth.

that spirituality involves *all* aspects of your being. The difficulty here for hard-nosed psychologists is that, as these two frames of reference merge, it becomes more and more difficult to define or measure the psychological data, and less and less possible to ignore the conviction that spiritual perspectives are valid, even if they can't be defined or measured.)

3   Nothing Is Not Spiritual

In this connection, a more general issue for some people is a tendency to divorce some parts of their lives from their spirituality: their sarcasm, overeating, fantasies, laziness and other human failings. The good news is that we stay human in spirituality no matter how far we get with it; what's challenging is that there is no part of our humanity

We STAY HUMAN in spirituality, no matter how far we get with it.

that does not undergo a searching inquiry and transformation, as you do your practices. As you work your way though these pages the conviction will dawn upon you (if it hasn't long since), that there is nothing, absolutely nothing in our lives which does not affect our spirituality or have a spiritual dimension.

A rough analogy can be drawn from the experience of drug addicts who recover successfully from their habits. It's common for the addict interested in recovery to start out thinking that certain parts of his or her life have nothing to do with their drug use. But they soon realize that everything they do—the people they spend time with, the food they eat, the amount and type

EVERYTHING you do impacts your spirituality.

of their activities and exertions, the things they say and think—it all impacts the degree of awareness and resolve they have at those crucial moments when, upon temptation, they decide whether or not to start using their substance again.

4 It *Can* Change Your Reality

Religion and spirituality are thought by some people to be merely wishful thinking. Perhaps it does create cheerful states of mind, they think, as well as the morals on which all good human conduct is based. But that's it. Their main contention might be that spirituality is useless against the laws of nature and the larger manifestations of human evil, and always has been. (This is especially the case with some *deistic* believers (Ch.6,S.3) who generally hold that divine intervention is quite rare.)

The main antidote to this is having an open mind and being willing to "examine the evidence," which in this case is more subjective, involving both introspection concerning our own minds, and admiration of some other peoples' minds. We end up admitting that we do envy those others' levels of personal fulfillment, and that they must see the world, somehow, in a "happier" way than we do, even though they remain intelligent.

How might your reality change if you had a better or worse attitude towards life than you do? For many people, the changes in their own lives suffice to support the idea that attitude does have a real impact. Others don't trust themselves that way. They benefit more from understanding the spiritual principles connected with those attitudes by which those changes are thought to come about, in conjunction with modern physics and psychology. This requires study, but it's worth it if you have trouble relating to more subjective material.

The idea "think and grow rich" is NOT quite complete nonsense.

Along these lines many books have been written on creativity and manifestation, which explain and help us apply spiritual laws to bring about beneficial changes. In a very real sense this is a science as well, since all the good writers in this area say the same things in different ways.[2] The idea of "think and grow rich" *does* have a grain of truth to it, although in a more sophisticated and mature way than

NISARGADATTA MAHARAJ—20th Cent. *tobacco merchant and later teacher, Mumbai, India. Author of influential transcribed volume* I Am That, *which brought him a worldwide following. His teachings remain important for secular-style seekers, as well as for traditional devotees of jnana yoga, the Hindu path of knowledge. Rendered from* I Am That *photo inset.*

most of us are aware of. At certain stages of the spiritual journey, it is possible to employ one's faith, intention and so forth to bring about changes in you life which otherwise would not occur (Ch.11,S.6).

An important thing to understand in this connection, finally, is that especially since the inception of Einstein's Theory of Relativity in the early 20th century, and that of Quantum Mechanics shortly there-after, the boundary between the terms "natural" and "supernatural" have blurred.[3] A growing body of popular, quasi-academic literature exists supporting the contention that these theories provide evidence for the subtle mechanisms through which spiritually-related phenomena take place, such as such as telepathy, prescient dreams or visions, hunches which turn out to be true and so on, as well as the classic spiritual powers described in mystical literature.[4] This

> *The planet is* WAKING UP—*and scientific support of mysticism is a major reason why.*

new, scientific support of mysticism may be the biggest factor contrib-uting to the spiritual awakening currently taking place on the planet.[5]

5 Everyone's A Mystic

This word brings all kind of images to mind, so we need some clarity as to what a mystic is. It's used in mostly two ways. The first is to refer to somebody who has spiritually-related powers and abilities, maybe above and beyond the average psychic. The other, more academic use is in connection with spiritual teachers in the religions who are presumably enlightened and experience union with God. Any renowned guru, master, sheikh, etc. is by definition also a mystic, although the term is not usually used in that way due to its association with psychic powers.

A third use of the term might be anyone who either reaches enlightenment or is serious about trying, and understands it to be something anyone can pursue, whatever our station in life might be. That's how we will think of it in this book.

6 Spiritual Evolution

Finally, spiritual evolution does exist, and people do change their practices, understandings and associations as they move along in their journey. For this reason, a duality runs through this book for instructional purposes. The main way this duality manifests is in the contrast between different basic stages of spiritual development. *Fundamentalist* or *orthodox* perspectives and experiences are discussed at one stage, and *mystical, profound,* or sometimes *liberal-minded* perspectives and experiences are discussed at the other stage. In some of the pictures, likewise, *superficial meaning* often contrasts with *profound meaning.* However, although this distinction has validity and is clear most of the time, neither of these positions can be defined and they clearly break down in some cases.

It's worth being DISRESPECTED if it makes you think!

While I don't mean to disrespect anyone, I do wish to stimulate a good bit of thinking and personal reevaluation, both for those who haven't thought about these things, as well as for those who've thought too much in unproductive ways. Again therefore, everybody is a mystic—at least potentially.

LABYRINTH—*Universal motif, most associated with Greek myth. Superficial meaning: place where one might get lost trying to do something in life. Profound meaning: mysterious, complex, unexpected and often arduous nature of path back to God/Self.*

CHAPTER TWO

Equal Vision: Embracing Theism And Atheism

Equal vision means seeing everyone in the same light. Many of us cannot imagine being atheistic, but we need an understanding of spirituality that embraces everyone, including atheists. How can enlightenment occur otherwise? Contemplating some basics concerning God's inscrutability (as we will also do later—Ch.3,S.1) provides us with this understanding.

Everyone is aware of this connection at some level. We're all in the same boat. If atheists are in denial about God, then in a sense believers are just as deluded concerning the nature of God, because God/Self, after all, *isn't anything* the senses can know or which the mind can fathom. We will be getting a better sense of this shortly.

1   Superficial Reasons For Atheism

Most reasons given by atheists for their lack of belief are not at all profound. Some of them are: 1) the bible doesn't always make sense and is often inconsistent, 2) God is described in contradictory ways, 3) the teachings of the religions are contradictory, 4) the gods described in the religions resemble human beings too closely to be plausible.

> *Most atheists' reasons for not believing involve* GRADE SCHOOL *level thinking.*

Such reasons imply that the person's understanding of religion is merely cultural, tied to superficial phenomena involving language and politics. If those things were all that religion was, then of course the atheists would be right. Such skeptics who end up getting something out of this book, however, will be radically rethinking their entire orientation to spirituality.

(I do a lot of atheist bashing in this chapter—not so in Chapter 3!)

2 Core Idealism, Spiritualities And The God Concept

All unenlightened humans possess what we can call a *core idealism*—their own, unique interior sense of perfection and beauty. That core idealism is not itself associated with any form. It is an abstract but felt combination of ethical and spiritual qualities. This is the closest thing to God/Self that most people are in touch with.

And we associate that core idealism with different things in our minds. To some degree, we associate it with *human experience and form*, allowing us to equate it with a kind of perfect, larger than life person: God. This basic idea[1] is common to people in all cultures. People who don't believe in God merely have different primary associations with their core idealism: philosophy, poetry, literature, music, drug use, science and technology, or—perhaps most commonly—friends and family.

> *RELIGIOUS spirituality is only the best-known type of spirituality. There are lots of others!*

From the monistic perspective, in which everyone returns to God/Self eventually, all these "choices" are different types of spiritualties. However, it is easy to see why *religious* spirituality, associated with the God-concept, is the most popular alternative worldwide. Whether or not the individual's spirituality involves teachers, spirituality has always manifested most powerfully though particular human beings, so most people ended up associating their core idealism, again, with "human form"—that is to say, with certain special teachers. That's how God became the most powerful and important of all universal archetypes.[2]

3 The Halfhearted Majority

This book is concerned with philosophical issues within religious spirituality. This particular chapter is concerned with seekers who are mostly *philosophical*, rather than religious, in their spirituality—who powerfully believe in certain notions

> *Like it or not, spirituality has always manifested most powerfully through* PARTICULAR HUMAN BEINGS.

that don't allow them to associate their core idealism with any of the great spiritual teachers. It also addresses believers who do not connect with their existing spiritual teachers like they want to, for similar reasons.

JOHN OF THE CROSS—16TH Cent. canonized Doctor of the Church, Spain. Co-founder of Discalced Carmelite order and famous for influential theological writings (primarily Ascent of Mt. Carmel (including Dark Night of the Soul). He wrote his greatest poetry while being imprisoned and frequently tortured by those resisting his reforms—later escaping out a window and sliding down a rope of bedclothes.

As was said before (Ch.1,S.1), in a very important sense, belief is experience. We can think of people as falling into four categories. *Full believers* are enlightened beings, and are still rather rare. When it comes to God, they have no doubt about anything since they have *become* him/her/it. Around 85 or 90% of us are *halfhearted believers* to some degree, plagued by some quantity of doubt since we're not enlightened. The more progress we make in our spirituality, the less halfhearted we become.

Insincere atheists—who I believe are the majority of them—comprise the third category. They can, with enough life experience, education and/or therapeutic intervention, be brought around. Until then, they are believers by proxy: admiring the virtues of certain other people, usually famous ones, whom they associate with

> *Most atheists can be brought around through appropriate (THERAPEUTIC) education and experience.*

their own core idealism, and who themselves often believe in God. Like other imperfect seekers, these atheists realize that their happiness is compromised by their issues, and are implicitly aware of greater possible levels of contentment they might achieve. You might say they *want* to believe, but somehow or other life has "burned" them too much to allow it.

True or *sincere atheists,* finally, aren't as subject to these musings and will dismiss their own profound experiences as subtle neurochemical phenomena. Such nano-mechanical explanations account for even the most admirable qualities connected with human nature. These individuals are attached to more subtle philosophical positions (see below) than the commonplace ideas that many of us reject as we grow up.

Finally, I count *agnostics* as reluctant believers, at the skeptical end of the *halfhearted majority* category above. Sympathy for

> *In one way or another, most atheists are BELIEVERS BY PROXY.*

the idea that God might exist stems from a certain openness in the person, which some atheists lack.

4   Central Reasons For Atheism And Doubt

Atheists run the gamut from positive to negative in their attitude towards God and religion. The thoughtful ones—often very kind and gentle in disposition—regard God as a metaphor or figure of speech for a kind of mythical father figure, which we project onto the universe in order to relate to fate or destiny in a personal way.[3] Less thoughtful atheists often make it fairly obvious that their own negative experiences are responsible for their lack of belief; frequently projecting resentment onto the world and seeing things that are not there.

Atheists will say many things in response to the question of why they don't believe, but if you ignore the personal and emotional aspects and can pin them down to deeper reasons, three positions emerge: 1) difficult or negative events in the world, whether humanly or naturally caused, 2) deserving, repeated prayers which go unanswered, and 3) the idea that the universe doesn't need a creator or governor, since the laws of nature account for everything.

5   What God Really Is

The first two of these atheist justifications are countered easily enough with good arguments. These arguments prevail because atheists' ideas of what God *should* be (if he existed) don't match the reality of what God is. If we are going to try to describe God/Self conceptually, atheists' ideas are way off the mark, in that they attribute *too much* humanity to him, in the normal sense of the term. And given that so many of us are stuck in human dramas, most believers are guilty of this as well.

> *Most atheists attribute TOO MUCH HUMANITY to their idea of God (if he/she/it existed).*

Such anthropomorphizing is natural enough—it's even accurate in the long run. Only enlightened beings, however, really know *what it means to be human* in the fullest sense. In the meantime, we need to start disabusing ourselves of certain ideas associated with being human in the usual, limited sense.

To avoid quoting prose and poetry forever, and to pinpoint the central notions that we need to rethink, we will only discuss a few of God's philosophical attributes that give atheists trouble. They all turn on one central truth: that reality is suspended between pairs of opposites. Hot/cold (supernova temperature/absolute zero) is one such pair, or dyad. Reality exists between these extremes of temperature. You might call temperature one *spectrum* of creation.

In the process of creation, we might say that God *expanded himself* along a large number of other spectra, or continua: solid/space, big/little, human/inhuman, *homo sapiens*/virus, good/evil, masculine/feminine, and so on. From the monistic perspective, these pairs are not separate concepts, but single continua. For example, the greatest good and the most heinous evil form a single spectrum, with different degrees of

> *Anthropomorphism is actually ACCURATE in the long run!*

17

Extreme evil is part of creation—we simply need to DEAL WITH IT.

good and evil along a sliding scale in between. Profoundly understood, that spectrum is *one thing*. In principle, "evil" is not separate from "good" any more than yin is from yang in Chinese thought. Only in the realm of imagination is it possible to isolate them completely.

This addresses the first atheist objection above. Someone who doesn't like extreme evil must acknowledge that it is part of the variety of creation, even if there isn't very much of it.

Another continuum is reliable/unreliable, with regard to three things: concepts, human behavior, and external events. Praying to God is an example of a dubious concept, at least in terms of getting things done. How often are prayers really answered in the way we would like to see? As far as behavior goes, people never come through 100% of the time—no examples are needed! External events, finally—the weather, the stock market, our health— also very often don't do what we want them to. So, the inherent unpredictability of the universe

The universe is NOT going to line itself up behind Joe Blow's request for a BETTER JOB!

is also part of the variety and spontaneity of creation.

This addresses the second atheist objection. Prayers are rarely answered in the way we would like to see, because divine intervention is not the order of the day but only the rare exception (Ch.6,S.3)

6   The Good—Evil Continuum: A Closer Look

If you still reject the existence of God on the basis of extreme evil—say, the raping and torture of small children—then we need to perceive more closely the essential connectedness of this behavior with the better end of the good-evil spectrum.

Scale A: Living Conditions

Let's look first at the variety of conditions under which children can be raised:

1 Both parents present, good role models, extra money, good diet, good physical health, good house, good neighborhood, good schools.

2 The same as #1 above, except only *sufficient* money.

3 The same as #2, except for *okay* diet.

4 The same as #3, except for *confining* house.

You get the idea. You could list another 100 or so scenarios, making the adjectives progressively worse for all the features, and then for fewer of the features, until you ended up with:

> *Here's where I try to DESTROY anyone's sentimental attachments!*

100. Terrible role models, crappy/insufficient diet, poor physical health, homelessness, terrible and dangerous neighborhood.

ABRAHAM—*Ancient (18th Cent. BCE) quasi-mythical 1st Patriarch of Judaism. According to Islam, he also built the first house around the Kab'bah (black stone) worshipped in Mecca. In the Book of Genesis, at God's command he ejected his handmaiden Hagar and his son Ishmael into the desert, predisposing many modern conservative Jews and Christians to think they were out of favor with God. This impression carries over to Islam in general, since Ishmael supposedly wandered into Arabia and (in some sense) fathered all Muslims. Rendered from* Abraham and the Angels *by Arent de Gelder.*

Scale B: Mental Health and Genetics

We all know that some children don't turn out well even with very good living conditions; inborn potentials obviously play a part. In order to describe a growing young person, in general terms descending alternatives might be:

1 Good attitude, good general behavior, considerate and helpful to others, good impulse control, excels academically.

2 Same as #1, except *polite* to others.

3 Same as #2, except *okay* impulse control.

Option 25 (or however many) might be:

25. Terrible attitude, awful general behavior, cruel to others, severe addictions, flunked elementary school.

It's not hard to imagine someone towards the bottom of both these scales raping and torturing small children.

The rigorous and bitter truth is that both these scales illustrate, in one sense, the variety and glory of God's creation already mentioned. That is what I mean by *essential connectedness*. The monistic paradigm embraces all of them. On the other hand the Heaven/Hell paradigm (Ch.7,S.4), which is dualistic, would draw a line somewhere and declare the good above to be from God and the bad below from the devil.

> *There is nothing seen, imagined, existing or nonexisting ANYWHERE that the monistic paradigm does not embrace!!*

We can be polite and wishy-washy with ourselves and in conversation with others about these philosophies. But at the end of the day, where do you fall? Which of these two world-views makes more sense?

7   Are True Atheists Right?

The third argument given for atheism above is more difficult to counter, because it is indeed true that in many mystical philosophies, it is God's very nature to create, meaning that creation always existed insofar as God always existed, therefore possibly rendering God *per se* superfluous.

> *If God's nature is to create, his non-existence becomes AT LEAST MORE PLAUSIBLE.*

In this view, it is valid to ask the question, *how were the mountains and the stars created*, but invalid to ask, *how was the universe created*. Basically, at that point you're asking the question of your own being instead of about something outside of your being, which renders it invalid.

Beyond that, we won't get into philosophical technicalities (which keep a fair number of people deluded who are attached to their intellects).

Sincere atheists are PROFOUNDLY DEFIANT, and attached to subtle concepts such as Occam's Razor[4].

But of course it does make sense to ask this question. It does carry weight to say that, just as we know that individual things undergo creation, so the universe did or does as well. Real maturity[5] involves accepting not only that reality is governed by laws of nature, but that it is also pervaded by a transcendent dimension beyond nature that is *responsible* for nature. This higher reality undergirds and usually blends smoothly with the laws of this reality, making things work out as they should in usually normal ways. Divine intervention is rare.

8   Atheism, Art And Enlightenment

Another thing needs to be pointed out. At the level of understanding the grand operations of the universe, true atheists can be naught but deterministic. At depth, they are hardnosed empiricists wedded to *deus ex machina*. At that level this has to be true. Science obviously amounts to something. How else can you explain the workings of the universe? Those atheists who are artists of some kind, who depend upon the creativity and inspiration mentioned above, must concede that their "gift" works purely scientifically. If it doesn't, what is the agency that determines the "spontaneous" time and manner in which your creativity manifests?

Really ENCOUNTER the question: is the universe deterministic?

To that you might answer, "I think you're wrong. That's not what the creative process feels like at all, at least for me. It's just something I can do well, that's all." That's fine—but you're dodging the question. Or rather, you're not really *encountering* the question, or engaging the mystery of what that gift is. You prefer a kind of surface-level answer.

Any true atheist rankled enough at this accusation will begin to think more deeply about the nature of reality. What are the mechanics

21

behind everyday, usually-taken-for-granted events and circumstances? If the supernatural does exist,[6] what is it based on? If a final and supreme enlightenment *doesn't* exist, in what sense is the term meaningful, and how far can it go?

The final argument against atheism presented here is one set forth elsewhere in more detail (Ch.5,S.1-4), which is basically that, as human beings, at least subconsciously[7] we *have* to believe in God/Self, since we are faced with an infinite, dangerous universe and must deal with that perception on some level. It is a circular[7] argument, but still may be convincing for more uncertain (agnostic) readers.

> *We have an EASIER TIME in life if we can derive meaning from something that is ABSOLUTELY PERMANENT!*

9   The Marks Of Existence

The Buddhist *religion* is no better than any other. The guy who started it, however, was exceptionally clear and pithy in his understanding. Atheists can also learn life's lessons due to the three **Marks of Existence**. They are, one, *impermanence*. Nothing lasts. Even the mountains and stars eventually crumble. Two, *suffering*. Grief, pain, disillusionments, hassles and disappointments are part and parcel of life. And three, *soullessness*. By this he meant that, although an ultimate reality exists, *it cannot be found* in any normal sense, either within or without. God is so profound that He/She/It may as well not exist (Ch.3,S1).

Understanding these truths results in wisdom and can lead to enlightenment. Believers have an easier time, however, since they are consciously aware of the goal and can derive meaning from it. Atheists must derive meaning from something that, by definition, is either transient and/or completely impersonal, since that thing cannot be God. Overall therefore, the atheist's journey through life involves more pain and confusion.

In one sense belief is not necessary: we all embody the grace of God and give glory to him, often without realizing it. We are not machines, however. Atheists should ponder the questions and issues above. True ones are sincere for having thought through and rejected at least their own understanding of the more subtle concepts of God connected with mysticism. For that reason, I consider them to be **monistic** and **panentheistic** believers (Ch.6,S.3), at least subconsciously.[8]

SERPENT IN TREE—*Superficial meaning: A snake climbing a tree (in the biblical Garden of Eden, it can talk as well). Profound meaning: any axis (maypole, caduceus, Christmas tree, spinal column) along which spiritual energy in its most classic metaphor can ascend and "blossom" in whatever way, transforming the body-mind which houses it.* From Emblems Divine and Moral, *by* Francis Quarles, *Artist Unknown.*

CHAPTER THREE

Questions
Surrounding Belief

This chapter will appeal to atheists more than the last one!

Although I will be speaking informally about "God" and related issues to most readers who do believe, nonbelief is not as big an obstacle to one's spirituality as you may be inclined to think. To better understand this, it's worth looking at some basic philosophical points about "belief," "enlightenment" and a few other terms.

1   Belief And Nonbelief In God (It Doesn't Matter)

The main reason the above is true is that whatever the Ultimate Reality is, it is utterly profound and absolutely unknowable in the usual sense—so much so that it almost may as well not exist (even the Buddha believed[1]). It exists anterior even to our ability to think about it. While some people don't believe in "God," they do acknowledge—by virtue of being human, if their attitude is mature—that this vast universe, in its sheer scale and mystery, contains an infinity of phenomena that we cannot possibly know or experience every-thing about. That very fact elicits an awe and humility to which we must, in a sense, submit. You don't have to call it or personalize it

> OBVIOUSLY the universe is not made of three places called "heaven," "hell." and "earth."

24

with a word or a name, but you do have to acknowledge "it" at some level, if you hope to develop a spirituality that is in any sense sincere.

Of those who count themselves agnostics, many do so only because the spiritual ideas they were exposed to were and remain basically geared towards children. That's organized religion! Everyone listening needs

> OBVIOUSLY *God is not any more male than female.*

to be able to relate to it at some level. So: in any of the more touchy-feely "God-talk" throughout this book, bear in mind that the Ultimate Reality described in the first paragraph above is the only one really being referred to. It's more a matter of faith than belief. If the mind insists on direct evidence, it will be sorely disappointed because there's nothing there to believe *in*.

> OBVIOUSLY *God does not endorse religious wars or think one religion is better than the others.*

At any rate, obviously, starting to outgrow such childish versions of God can be disorienting, if that's what we've been listening too all our life at our place of worship.

2 Being Lost (Not Knowing What You Believe)

There are three situations in which people don't know what's going on in their spiritual life. The first comes about simply from never having thought about it—which is to say, it doesn't make sense to them at the level of knowledge and interest they currently have. The second situation is "losing faith"—that is, encountering discouraging things in the world (evil, wars, etc.), which God, at least in the person's conception, would never do. The third situation is more profound, and involves reaching a kind of impasse, usually after having made a lot of progress without realizing it. In this process, some people work out their issues with God to the point where they no longer have any agenda of their own: no more personal hang-ups which predispose them to believe one way or another (Ch.5,Int.). As a result they find themselves at loose ends, not knowing what to think.

> *Many of us have simply never given SERIOUS THOUGHT to spiritual issues.*

Which, or which combination of these applies to you? Everyone is different. If it's a matter of thinking about it, this book can help lead you through that process. If it's a matter of discouragement or disgust, hopefully it will help explain the inevitability of various profound things (i.e., evil), which should motivate further contemplation, since true maturity doesn't allow us to ignore such things (Ch.10,S.6). For an impasse, perhaps it will help you find a new and constructive direction.

SHEIKH NAZIM—20-21ˢᵗ Cent. Sufi Master, Cyprus (d. 2014). Nazim travelled widely, admired European civilization, made a number of failed apocalyptic predictions and declared G.W. Bush and Tony Blair "saints" in Islam for their crusade against evil in their invasion of Iraq. Although generally a mystical group, some of his 30-40 million Sufi followers seem to hold exclusivist attitudes concerning Nazim's greatness.

3   Beliefs And Attitude

Encountering spiritual concepts with wrong attitudes is another issue, affecting perhaps a majority of seekers. You may have just read or listened politely, since you were already sold on your own ideas without realizing it.

Cynicism is pervasive in our culture. Many of us are conditioned this way more deeply than we think we are. Much of the news and entertainment industries are based on three key human failings: 1) our susceptibility to flattery, as when someone implies that we're smart about this and that and therefore, we should identify with their product or group; 2) susceptibility to prideful superiority, as

> *Most people watch TV merely with a MORE SUBTLE VERSION of the mindset the romans had while watching their gladiators.*

when almost everyone on TV or video intentionally makes fools out of themselves in order to get us to like them, and 3) susceptibility to exaggeration and gossip, as when actors perform impossible feats in movies or cut each other down.

Some of this is merely a more subtle version of the gladiator mentality back in the Roman Empire, when people shouted and screamed for blood when people or animals they didn't like were being slaughtered. We must put aside such failings. Feelings of superiority and assumptions of falsehood everywhere render us jaded, unwilling to take a second look at ideas either dismissed as nonsense or never really learned in the first place. Spirituality is about *reality,* not myth, although myth is important for many people (Ch.5,S.6). It pays for all of us to be more receptive to old ideas when they are presented well, and under favorable conditions.

> *Haven't most of us outgrown beliefs such as SANTA CLAUS COMING DOWN THE CHIMNEY on Christmas Eve?*

4   Types Of Belief, And Literal Belief As An Obstacle

Central to understanding religion is appreciating why different people often believe the same thing in different ways. It may not be appropriate to judge others externally, but we need to do so for ourselves if we are to find our own way.

Due to people's varied conditionings, there's actually a spectrum of ways to believe a given doctrine, but for clarity's sake I'll describe the three most general categories. *Literal* or *fundamentalist* belief involves understanding things "word-for-word"—that is, only according to the most obvious and apparent meaning of the terms being used. So some people, for example, think that God created the universe in six days—period—as the Book of Genesis in the bible says. Then there's *partially metaphorical/allegorical* belief, in which not everything is taken literally; the individual follower decides for him- or herself

> *Literal believers are the ones responsible for all the WARS AND ARGUMENTS.*

how to interpret things he doesn't choose to believe in literally. In the Christian Gospels, for example, one believer might decide that the manger animals really were the first creatures to worship Jesus, but consider too fanciful the notion that angels came down from heaven to announce his birth. Another believer might assess this differently. Finally, there is *mystical* belief, in which the goal of the spiritual quest is the only important thing. The routes many take to get there—the various religions—are all just "stories." One's as good as the next.[2] To a mystic, *everything* in reality is metaphorical since nothing but God is permanent.

> *Since it necessarily involves literalism, much of public discourse on religion sounds like a PLAYGROUND SQUABBLE.*

Being the most inflexible, literal believers are the ones responsible for all the wars and arguments involving religion. Political parties and national institutions favor the literalist version of their cultures' faiths, for the same reason most places of worship do: because everybody needs to be able to relate to what they are saying on some level, since the population of any country contains some immature adults, as well as children. For many educated, liberal-minded believers who have given these issues some thought, this type of belief is exasperating and privately imbecilic. Most all of us with Christian backgrounds outgrow the belief that Santa Claus comes down the chimney on Christmas Eve to deliver presents. Some of the literalist spiritual beliefs around which wars are fought have similar content.

(Actually, as we explore the human capacity for enlightenment and what it involves later in the book, we'll see that such events conceivably *can* happen (Ch.5,S.6), although by any account there is significant immaturity involved in using such beliefs as a basis for warfare.)

5   Believing In Enlightenment (It Does Exist)

The idea of enlightenment gives a lot of people trouble. First, let's examine the term.

People use the word *enlightenment* in three ways: 1) learning more about a particular topic or topics, so that you become a better person overall, perhaps all the way up to what some psychologists call *self-actualization* (S.7), 2) having a spiritual awakening of some kind, often followed by similar experiences, but nevertheless leaving you incompletely fulfilled, and 3) what we can generically call *true spiritual enlightenment,* which does represent a state of complete fulfillment.

> *The idea that we are all POTENTIAL JESUS CHRISTS is simply too radical for most people.*

BLACK ELK—*Early 20ᵗʰ cent. Ogalala Lakota teacher and medicine man. He had an eleven-day vision at age 9, participated in the battle of Wounded Knee and authored the transcribed volume* Black Elk Speaks. *He traveled with Buffalo Bill's Wild West Show in United States and Europe, and saw similarities between Christianity and Sioux religion—enough to became a Catholic Catechist later in his life, in spite of the Church's oppression of Native Americans.*

I say "generically" because the religions use different terms to describe this state. A Christian might call it *Christ-consciousness,* a Hindu might say *moksha* (liberation), a Sufi might say *fana* (annihilation in God), and Buddhist and Buddhist-oriented secular groups—of which there are many—might call it being *awake,* or *enlightened.* If you're coming out of a humanistic psychology background, you might say *self-realization.* But these are just words. The actual inner experience or state of being to which they point is the object of our inquiry here. Is it the same for everybody? It has to be; otherwise you're privileging one group over another (see Ch.4). At any rate, most of the time, the word used in this book is *enlightenment.*

> *Enlightenment would NOT render us all depersonalized robots.*

This enlightenment is conceptually problematic. It claims to represent a final state of complete fulfillment based on an existing ultimate reality, which is the same for everybody. As such,

29

enlightenment implies total perfection and uniformity, both of which seem to be "inhuman," allowing no room for the uniqueness that makes each of us precious in the eyes of God/Self. It seems we would all end up becoming depersonalized robots.

6 Basic Arguments For Elightenment And Monism

Because of all the ways that enlightenment is paradoxical (such as: you remain an imperfect human being), it is impossible to present solid evidence that cannot be plausibly interpreted in a way that does not support the notion. But there are some classic arguments in favor of it that can be briefly stated. They are also arguments for the existence of God.

Many would be uncomfortable admitting out loud that enlightenment MIGHT BE REAL.

The first of these arguments addresses the tendency to intentionally not define or qualify spirituality in any way. Because people's attitudes and orientations about it are so diverse, because religions, sects and practices can seem so different, some people think that there isn't—at least practically speaking—a goal to the spiritual quest. In this view, "spirituality" (whatever that really is) unfolds and go on forever, endlessly mysterious and alluring, but never quite offering complete fulfillment.

The third form of enlightenment mentioned above—the one we're focusing on in this book—doesn't exist in this way of thinking; if God is thought to exist at all, he does so *deistically* (Ch.6,S.3), since he can't be attained. The upshot of all this points to what I like to call the *Constructive Delusion Theory* of religion and mysticism: that although the religions have been helpful, even essential, in human history, in the end they are our own subconscious creations for the sake of law and order, having no basis in reality (Ch.7,S.7).

At any rate, to address these objections, the first argument I present here isn't really an argument. It merely presents the sheer historical and intellectual

FEIGNED IGNORANCE stemming from god's ineffability is a major act of SPIRITUAL COWARDICE.

weight of human conviction, based on faith and experience, which asserts three things: 1) God *can* be contacted or united with; 2) sainthood, past and present, *does* exist; and 3) there *is* a goal or endpoint to the spiritual jour-

> *For the sake of faith, TAKE A STAND: is there a goal, or not?*

ney. These claims imply that enlightenment in the mystical sense as defined above does exist. Without them, any given concept of enlightenment is vague, open to greater possible fulfillment than that connected with the one you currently hold. Anyone can claim enlightenment. At some point, however, you must draw a line, which distinguishes between the enlightenment of union with God and other senses of the word.

Another argument involves the traditional criteria by which we used to think of ourselves as different from all other animals. This is the capacity for sentience, or self-awareness. Recently however, investigations of some individual apes' and dolphins' degree of mastery of complex sign-language communication, and their obvious feeling-based responses of grief, sympathy, etc. imply levels of self-awareness we never imagined they had. Some species of birds have likewise recently demonstrated extraordinary reasoning ability and power of memory. So if you insist on there being some fundamental difference between us and other animals, it can't, again, be a

> *For our fulfillment to be supreme and permanent, we must UNDERSTAND LIFE, instead of just living it.*

greater potential *degree* of enlightenment, otherwise *homo sapiens* is merely the best mousetrap, as it were, that God ever built. There needs to be a distinction—the same one mentioned above. Some sort of goal or fulfillment has to exist to correspond to an absolute distinction between us and other animals. (We don't know for sure that other species of animals can't attain the same final enlightenment as we can, but it's a reasonable assumption.)

It is useful to briefly restate some basic assumptions and distinctions that both these arguments make. If we grant that 1) God exists, and 2) that God does communicate or make himself known to us, then uniting with God completely must be possible. This is because if He/She/It only communicates partially with us, than there is room for doubt that that communication is authentic, precisely because it isn't possible to know God completely and absolutely, meaning that what is communicating with us could conceivably be something else. God might not even exist.

The next question involves what these arguments imply about your own priorities.

7   Are You Interested?

This can be a very powerful question to contemplate, in relation to one's priorities in life. If you 1) believe in God, 2) believe that human beings are special in their ability to know him, 3) believe that that ability is shared by all human beings, 4) want a

> *EVEN SOME ANTS AND BIRDS are halfway sophisticated in the way they go about things like food storage and courtship.*

more fulfilled life, and 5) want that fulfillment to be supreme and permanent, then you are interested in enlightenment.

The fifth item above is the kicker. What are human beings for? Are we really just that "best mousetrap" who reproduces, builds shelters and (although it somewhat sophisticated ways) brings home the bacon like other animals? If so, we shouldn't be bothering with so-called spiritual enlightenment.

Part of us, however, *is* interested, in spite of the tendency we often have to think that we're "not ready."

8   Real *Spiritual* Maturity

The question of readiness involves understanding maturity in the psychological sense, and contrasting that with one of the paradoxes connected with enlightenment.

It is possible to think about enlightenment systematically, but only up to a point. In the psychological frame of reference, it stands to reason that *self-actualization* (a term out of humanistic psychology) is a prerequisite for enlightenment, since self-actualization represents the peak development of human life in normal terms—family, career, pleasures, aesthetic fulfillment and so on. If that were true, however, there would be *a system to God.* We could use existing

> *Enlightenment represents an ABSOLUTE BREAK from psychology as we usually think of it.*

measures of psychological maturity to figure out how close we are to it, and whether or not we're ready to seriously pursue it. But it doesn't work that way. There are cases of enlightenment occurring among either very young people[3] as well as in people who, by all appearances, were wrestling with significant psychological issues that would certainly not seem to indicate truly mature levels of development.

What this tells us is that, the indices by which we might measure psychological maturity are ultimately invalid, and that enlightenment represents an *absolute break* from mainstream psychology as we normally think of it, even though psychological maturity is obviously involved most of the time. What all this means is that the highest human potential and fulfillment is an absolute mystery.

> *The best spiritual teachings today happen OUTSIDE THE RELIGIONS, since teachers don't have to be humble followers.*

So this is one of the confounding things you hear again and again from the great teachers, although usually expressed indirectly: you don't have to be mature or experienced enough in the world to qualify for self-realization,[4] and there's nothing anyone can do to guarantee that they'll attain it. As the most sentient creatures on the planet, by definition God exists within us and we're always trying to get back to him, however covered over that desire may be, and we cannot deny that possibility to anyone.

9 *How* Are You?

There is a way that most of us can get at least a basic sense of how "ready" or interested we are. Two things separate us from other animals: our capacity for enlightenment and the unique capacity we have for learning. There are some basic stages in life we can look at to get a sense of this: 1) growing out of childhood (acknowledging the value of open-mindedness and learning), 2) basic proficiency in the world (a sense of one's occupation or calling), and

> *There are ways you can GAUGE HOW READY you are, mature or not.*

3) the capacity for true intimacy (ability to have long-term special relationships).[5]

GOBIND SINGH—*18th Cent. Sikh leader and last in their line of Gurus. He orchestrated perhaps the most powerful and dramatic religious ceremony ever: pretending to behead five low-caste followers behind a curtain—showing a bloodied sword to his audience from a slain goat—then revealing them "reborn" and dressed in finery. He went on to initiate them into the new Khalsa Military Society, and—in front of everyone—knelt down as the Guru and had them initiate him.*

Practically speaking, all three of these are prerequisites for self-realization, in spite of what the teachers seem to say about not always having to be mature. If the seeker's interest in enlightenment is there, however, it doesn't matter whether the person has done these three things or not. In some cases, that strong interest results in what's usually referred to as a *spiritual bypass*[6]—in which spiritual concepts and experiences possess the person strongly enough to blind him or her to maturity deficits that may be obvious to others. (If that's your path, so be it—at some point, others will make you aware of your personal issues, and you'll be forced to catch up later.)

> *EVERYONE SELF-ACTUALIZES, however slowly or glacially in some cases.*

Beyond these first three qualifying stages is a fourth, which we might call *involuntary philosophizing*. This happens to everyone, because all human being grow and eventually start perceiving deeper things about reality, whether they want to or not (Ch.10,S.6). This is usually accompanied by a gradual loss of interest in former priorities. What makes this different from more typical midlife crises, however, is that the person is at more of a complete loss about what to do or think next.[7] This fourth stage doesn't always happen, because some people find their spiritual path at a lesser level of overall maturity, in which case the spiritual path functions as a kind of parent, for good or for bad (Ch.12,S.3&4). In these instances seekers have at least some of their confusions alleviated as they are going through them.

10 Normal Folks Can Get There

Enlightenment is not something that can be achieved only by certain rare individuals. If you spend enough time looking through the spiritual litera-ture in different cultures, you'll run across many cases of obscure individuals who became enlightened,[8] and there are many obscure or otherwise normal people today to whom it seems to be happening.[9]

MORE PEOPLE THAN EVER report radical and transformative "waking up" experiences outside any "spiritual" context.

Also, we can all do spiritual practices. These are the mechanics and technology of inner transformation. They open us to deeper reality, causing us to learn things much more quickly than ordinary life would otherwise take to teach. The teachers all say that they draw the grace of God.

The third encouraging point for "the average person" to be made here involves reincarnation (Ch.7,S.5), which is accepted, in one way or another, by basically all followers of Eastern and indigenous faiths, and by substantial numbers of people in the Western faiths.[10] What teachers often say in so many words (usually by telling stories) strongly endorses the "old soul" cliché—that a person may have done lots of thinking and practice in previous lifetimes.

The problem many people have with reincarnation, of course, is that there is no well-documented direct evidence to support it, at least according to mainstream science. By direct evidence I mean something like, well-documented cases of young people speaking languages or recalling events that did take place and which they could not possibly have learned since birth. Seeker curious enough about this will find, however, that the anecdotal evidence for this is fairly common and often compelling. It's probably safe to say that evidence for reincarnation, as for other paranormal

> PRACTICALLY NOTHING *in mystical spirituality is absolutely true or absolutely false.*

things like psychokinesis and the like, "intentionally manifest" only in intellectual atmospheres that are accepting of them, and where people would benefit from being exposed to them. This of course is the very antithesis of the laboratory conditions insisted upon by empirical science.

11 Limitations Of Belief

This is only a book, and some people don't learn things primarily through their intellect. Truth is beyond the mind; life and spiritual practice only prepare the intellect for its final, self-transcendent leap. But

> *The Abrahamic single-lifetime theory* ALSO *has things going for it.*

most people, although they may have gained profound understandings about God through normal life, haven't used their minds as much as they'll eventually need to.

"Gray areas" often characterize life. It is impossible to label a human being, for example, absolutely good or evil, because of the great variety of physical, biological, social, and economic factors that can impact and shape him or her (Ch.2,S.6). Higher reality is even more complex and manifold. For example, it's probably more accurate to say that reincarnation is *significantly* true, rather than absolutely so. The profound concepts which it helps many seekers to ponder are always fuzzy and ambiguous.

PART 2

PHILOSOPHICAL UNDERSTANDINGS

Many great teachers tell us—especially Siddhartha Gautama, the guy who started Buddhism—that topics like creation, the afterlife, theories of religion, whether or how God judges us, the possibility and mechanics of reincarnation and so on should be of secondary importance to anyone with a strong interest in enlightenment. Such information is irrelevant, they say, to maintaining the actual practices and attitudes that get you there.

For some, however, a major impetus for pursuing spirituality is the aesthetic and philosophical appeal of some of the ideas connected with mystical worldviews, and how these views make more sense than others in understanding how everything works. We might also pursue spirituality due to our complaints and misgivings about organized religion—not recognizing its purpose, and the inevitable reasons for its existence.

Once this is understood and the concept of enlightenment makes more sense, we can fruitfully compare and contrast paradigms to clear up certain questions, put in perspective numerous valuable ideas, and settle on the particular combination of more profound viewpoints that resonates with us.

SWASTIKA—*Universal motif; Hindu version. Superficial meaning: Earth element, auspiciousness, four directtions, etc. Profound meanings: "big bang" reverse vortex, creation emerging from God; incarnation process, unwinding of kundalini. Courtesy Wikimedia Commons.*

CHAPTER FOUR

Refutation Of Orthodox Thought

Before we delve into more universal and mystical perspectives, we need to dispose, once and for all, of attachment to orthodox perspectives. These ideas are fine for many people. While externally, most such people do not contribute to the wars and arguments caused by these doctrines, psycho-spiritually it can be argued that they do. Just as the child of a drug addict will instinctively discern that something is wrong (and therefore end up confused) even if the parents hide the problem, subtle tensions created by rigid beliefs help perpetrate sociopolitical conflicts involving religion on the surface.

1   How Arguments Can Help

There are two parts to this chapter. Under *Discursive Arguments* I present some primarily sociological polemics explaining why groups of people are the way they are. These arguments all take issue with beliefs in the special-ness of certain people, which cannot be entirely disproved since they are based on faith. Essentially what arguments like this do is appeal to the fact that, in

LEGALITIES ARE TIRESOME in life because they DOCUMENT OBVIOUS THINGS, such as the wrongness or murder and rape. So IT IS WITH THESE ARGUMENTS in spirituality.

order to make sense of anything, we have to understand most things in life systematically, and that understanding spiritual issues in that way is preferable to accepting teachings (of possibly mythical content) simply because they have the weight of tradition and authority behind them.

> *The laws of nature are OMNIPRESENT—just like the mystic's perception of God.*

Then, some very simple *Linguistic Deconstructions* are presented, illustrating some of the consequences of interpreting basic teachings in different ways. Although I am not a professional in the field, readers will get a sense in this section of what philosophers have long since done with the claims made in many religious texts. This last section of the chapter applies some very basic principles of *epistemology*—the formal study of knowledge itself, which involves grammar.

Many people are in the process of figuring out these truths on their own, in a more informal way. Hopefully this systematic material will benefit some readers. Scientific interpretations cannot represent the truths experienced in enlightenment, but they do provide the foundation for them. Rational understanding does provide a deeper, more durable faith than that of believers wedded to one version or other of some scriptural story.

DISCURSIVE ARGUMENTS

2 Because Growth Is Possible, There Are No God-Ordained Absolute Differences In Spiritual Capacity Between Two Different Groups Of Human Beings, Especially Of The Same Age And Culture

A prime tenant of fundamentalist religion seems to be that there are three categories of human beings: those who qualify to be with God after death, those who don't, and great prophets (a small subset within the God-qualifiers). We will deal with the first two of these groups immediately below, and then discuss the prophets in the next argument.

The first point to be made is that unlike the difference between man and other animals, the first two categories of humans mentioned above are closely related, since those who don't qualify to be with God after death can so qualify, merely by choosing to profess a new faith (or a different sect within the same faith). Clergy in these groups may tell us that God, not the individual, makes that choice, but this is belied by their own repeated exhortations that we should choose to accept their faith. And everybody knows from numerous examples

> *It is PATENTLY ABSURD THAT A UNIVERSAL GOD would choose to arrange things the way fundamentalists think.*

that according to the criteria of their own scriptures, the behavior of many fundamentalists does little to distinguish them even from many nonbelievers.

Moreover, while it is certainly true that God manifests different levels of intelligence and self-awareness in different people, it is dubious that there are measurable average differences of these kinds between similar groups of people from the same culture and local community. Therefore, attendees of fundamentalist and non-fundamentalist branches of the same faith within that area are very unlikely to have such differences. So it is highly unlikely that subtle

> *The more loud and strident a preacher is, the more certain we can be that HE HATES BOTH HIMSELF AND GOD.*

measureable factors unknown to science, and common to members within each group, exist that distinguishes the groups.

The possibility cannot be ruled out that nonmeasurable differences in intelligence, etc. might exist between these groups, due to God. This is very unlikely, however, for the reasons already stated: 1) the complete lack of measurable differences between the groups, 2) the fact that the difference between them can be bridged (and God's will countermanded) through simple choice of faith, and 3) the comparably poor behavior of the worst fundamentalists to that of the worst nonbelievers.

3   There Are No God-Ordained Absolute Differences In Spiritual Capacity Between So-Called Great Prophets And Other Human Beings

It can seem that so-called great prophets are qualitatively different human beings in some way. According to the western faiths, although hundreds

Everyone has a PROPHETIC DIMENSION to who they are, which they may or may not choose to develop.

of prophets have been sent to different civilizations throughout history, there is a small subset of great prophets, who delivered messages destined to reach all mankind. According to the Western faiths, there are very few such prophets—Abraham, Moses, Jesus, Muhammad and a few others (Islam, for example, claims there to be seven of them). We'll say a maximum of ten.

NEEM KAROLI BABA—*20ᵗʰCent. former family man and later ascetic, India. Through his various famous disciples (such as Ram Dass) who became authors, teachers, musicians, and healers, Neem Karoli has probably had a greater influence on the western world than any other Indian Guru, even though he never left the country.*

In this argument we examine the human being on the individual level, biologically and psychologically, instead of on the group level as in the first argument above. Again, the claim essentially is made that a truly qualitative difference does exist in some way between great prophets and other humans—they are, in other words, a different species.

But it is extraordinarily unlikely that great prophets constitute a second species of human, for the following reasons. First, there are so few of them; a different variety of human would certainly have reproduced to a greater number. Second, many of them were able to reproduce with ordinary humans and have descendants who were ordinary humans. Third, even if you grant that great prophets can be descendants of a great prophet father and an ordinary human mother (or vice versa), it seems unlikely that

We DON'T NEED TO INVOKE DIVINE FAVOR to explain the "greatness" of a particular prophet.

God would specially gift every such descendant as a great prophet, because there need be only a very small number of them to deliver messages to all humankind (see below).

A final argument against great prophets constituting a second type of human promotes the idea that great prophecy can develop as a personal gift. Five things can be said to be true: 1) people have different gifts, 2) the extent to which that gift gets

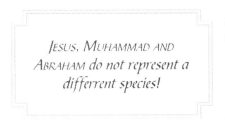

Jesus, Muhammad and Abraham do not represent a different species!

developed and expressed varies with the person, 3) personal and spiritual breakthroughs to greater levels of maturity and development often unlock a latent or repressed gift that a person has, 4) a very small number of individuals exist who have the very greatest development and expression of that gift, and finally 5) among this latter, already small group, social and historical circumstances will enable only a select few to utilize their gifts to extraordinary effect, spreading their teachings over the entire globe.

All this reinforces the truth that there is only one kind of human, and that things can naturally work out to account for ten prophets out of hundreds having the greatest spiritual influence. Therefore an external God is not necessary to transform select individuals into a different species for the sake of top-notch prophecy.

4   God Is Not A Human Being

The third argument concerns the nature of God. A prime tenant of fundamentalist religion is that the "word of God" as presented in the scriptures of a given faith is just that—the word of God. What is meant here is that, in effect, God is believed to have been a human being, since human beings spoke or wrote the words in question. Fundamentalist clergy in the religions will deny this, saying that God is infinitely great, unknowable and so on, but this is belied by their behavior and exhortations, to the effect that God's word should always be obeyed according to its simple,

Scriptures don't fall out of the sky.

"The kingdom of heaven is within you" is one line that fundamentalists SHY AWAY FROM TRYING TO EXPLAIN!

straightforward meaning in ordinary human terms. The strong implication of this, again, is that the humans who wrote or spoke the words in question are somehow God.

It seems, moreover, that if fundamentalist authorities really believed that God is vast, unknowable and whatnot, they would acknowledge that any words from a human being cannot possibly represent God in the absolute sense. Instead, the words would involve the cultural and linguistic context, as well as the individual conditioning, of the human writers. (Naturally, this would open the way for other interpretations of the words in question than the ones that fundamentalists favor.) Claiming that a special category of human can *be* God is, as Spinoza said in a related context, like equating the constellation of the dog in the night sky with the dog that barks.[1] Therefore human beings cannot be God.[2]

What follows is our basic linguistic analysis. For conservatives, the statements examined below justify the idea that God uniquely favors their religion. Each statement is followed by a structural analysis that clarifies the more systematic interpretations that mystics would favor.

LINGUISTIC DECONSTRUCTIONS

5 I Am The Way

This statement from the Gospels is attributed to Jesus Christ. Grammatically, it has a subject ("I"), and an object ("the way").

Possible Referents of "I"

1 Christ as a normal person

2 Christ as the unique Son of God

3 The knowledge of Christ; everything he knew or understood intellectually.

4 The innermost experience of God that Jesus Christ had, which transcended his body and personality.

Possible Referents of "the way"

1 A path to heaven, or God.

2 Physically being around Jesus as much as possible—either with him when he was alive, or with the remnants or representations of him (found in churches) since his death.

3 Following Jesus' teachings, whether you are physically with him or representations of him, or not.

Concerning "I," it is important to note that if Jesus is assumed to be a normal person, then options 3 and 4—the knowledge and inner experience he had—can be had by other persons as well.

All things in nature REPEAT THEMSELVES.

Concerning "the way," notice that if option 1 is not exclusively associated with Christ, than anyone with the requisite ability can help you get to heaven. And notice that option 2 ends up promoting the value of organized religion: valuing Christ as a guru or cult figure while he was alive, and (more importantly today) encouraging people to have formal gatherings around something that represents him (statues and pictures in churches) in death. Finally, note that option 3 is more difficult to fulfill than option 2: merely going to church does not make one a good Christian.

ANIMAL POPULATIONS ALWAYS HAVE more than one individual in them.

Aside from what was said above about so-called great prophets, a basic insight from modern science also argues against the possibility that Jesus Christ was a unique human being. This is that all things in nature repeat themselves. The components of a thing may mix together in different ways, but the objects themselves

An EXTRATERRESTRIAL THEORY is more plausible than the fundamentalist one-of-a-kind theory, since in that case JESUS WOULD REPRESENT AN ENTIRE RACE.

are each similar to one other. Each rock, for example, is unique in its size and shape, and may be composed of different quantities and proportions of various minerals—but they're all rocks. The rarest of all elements, iridium, occurs in quantities greater than a single atom. So all phenomena repeat themselves, including *Homo Sapiens*. Again, if there were another species of human of which Christ was an example, there would have to be more than one of them.

JUNPO DENIS KELLY ROSHI—*20-21ˢᵗ Cent. former felon (for dealing hallucinogens) and Founder of the Hollow Bones Zen Order, Wisconsin, USA. Ignoring his teacher's contention that "there is no Zen outside of Japanese culture," Junpo was influenced by the Mankind Project (MKP) to integrate modern psychology into traditional Rinzai koan format.*

Because of all this, some Christians believe Christ to have been basically a normal human being. Christians who do not accept this, and who do think Christ is unique, must own up to believing that Christianity is indeed the greatest and one true religion.

6 Jews Are The Chosen People

This basic understanding arose from the special treatment the Hebrew people received from God throughout the Old Testament. The subject here is "Jews" and the object is "the chosen people." Here's a breakdown:

Referents for "Jews"

1 The Jewish people.
2 All people who attain the same spiritual standing (moral/ethical quality as a person) that Jews do.

Referents for "the chosen people"

1 The ethnic/tribal group who received the Torah from God at Mt. Sinai.

2 All people whose behavior exemplifies the same level of moral/ethical quality that Jews manage to attain, in their efforts to live up to the Torah.

There has never been a case of virtually EVERYONE IN AN ENTIRE ETHNIC GROUP *feeling happy and blessed!*

Muhammad is NEVER PICTURED due to his association with God. Orthodox children's books in the faith portray him as a BLANK SPACE!

Concerning "the chosen people," many modern Jews accept option 2. The major supporting evidence for this is the point made above about phenomena in nature not being unique. Ethnic groups are ethnic groups, and there's no objective evidence to suggest that God favors any one of them.

Another point can be made here about "chosenness." Among all spiritually inclined people who do feel blessed and have had spiritual awakenings, it is indeed common to feel "chosen" in an individual sense, insofar as most people around him or her do not seem to be as happy or enlightened. Again however, this is on the level of the individual. All populations have individuals in them who are immature, sick, criminal, or otherwise unfortunate. For all these reasons, Jews who continue to believe option 1 must, again, own up to believing that Judaism is indeed the greatest and one true religion.

7   Muhammad Is The Seal Of The Prophets

In this metaphorical statement, Muslim teachers summarize their understanding of Muhammad's uniqueness. The term *seal* indicates the lid, top or covering of something. The thrust of Qur'anic teaching is that Muhammad is the last true prophet because enough people around him were finally able to understand the entire message God wanted to deliver to humankind. This was not the case with other great prophets, such as Jesus and Moses, who came before him.

The subject in this case is "Muhammad," and the object is "the seal of the prophets." Here's the breakdown:

Referents for "Muhammad"

1 A prophet who lived in 7th century Arabia.

2 A prophet who lived in 7th century Arabia who was indeed the last great messenger, to whom God delivered a uniquely comprehensive message.

Referents for "the seal of the prophets"

1 A metaphorical but accurate description of Muhammad, who was indeed the last great prophet and messenger, as stated above.

2 A metaphorical embellishment associated with Muhammad, added by early Muslim teachers who wanted to promulgate and spread the idea that Muhammad was privileged among prophets insofar as he was the one who delivered God's final and greatest message.

Again, on the basis of no natural phenomena being unique in nature, many modern Muslims accept option 1 for "Muhammad" and option 2 for "the seal of the prophets." Muslims who accept the other choices must own up to believing that Islam is indeed the greatest and one true religion.

> *Believe it or not, among major religious leaders,* M*UHAMMAD WAS THE WORLD'S FIRST FEMINIST.*[3]

HEBREW MENORAH—*Superficial meaning: oil miracle of Hanukkah. Profound meaning: progressive illumination of spiritual faculties, of sephirot on the Kabbalistic Tree of life. Courtesy Wikimedia Commons.*

CHAPTER FIVE

What Mysticism Is Not: The Structure Of Religion

Because they are profound, understanding mystical perspectives in spirituality more often involves realizing what they *are not*, rather than what they are. (Words can only hint at what those things *are*.) In the intellectual realm, as your journey continues, less and less attention is paid to factual and external circumstances and more attention to internal feelings, intuitions and guidance. This chapter details what most mystically inclined people sooner or later begin to understand, in one way or another, about religion—and organized religion in particular.

1 The Religious Seeker's Dilemma

Many seekers are no longer bothered by or care much about their religious backgrounds. They've gotten over the misleading notions that cause such turmoil among the faiths (Ch.4,S.4-6, also Ch.3,S.4). They realize that Jews are not "chosen" by God, that Christ is not "the only" son of God, that Muhammad is not "the seal" of the prophets, and that the Hindu *Atman/ Brahman*, the Buddhist *Nirvana*, and

> We need to OUTGROW RELIGION, insofar as religions are merely cultural expressions of profound truths that TRANSCEND CULTURE.

the Chinese *Tao* are not the only profound understandings of Ultimate Reality. Others, however, are tormented by these and similar issues, and need to work through them as best they can.

It is not possible to fully appreciate the internal differences between how mystically inclined seekers verses other kinds of seekers perceive and understand religion, without first understanding as best as we can why religions exist in the first place, and the psychological and existential functions which they serve. Religions, or at least a basic religious vocabulary, provide structures of beliefs and customs that accommodate the levels of interest of a majority of a culture's population. As we shall see, this is true whether the individuals involved are religious or not.

Understand these structures well enough, and you start to see the truth underneath them all.

2   Origins—The Infinite Scary Universe

The mystical explanation of the origin of religion is basically that because each of us already *is* God, *is* the universe, and because God/Self *hid itself from itself* in the process of creation, we vaguely sense all this and invent philo-

> *The humility inspired by modern knowledge of the* cosmos is SCIENCE'S GREATEST SPIRITUAL BENEFIT.

sophical and social systems to shield and buffer ourselves from the overwhelming magnitude of that experience, and to get closer to it in measured doses, if we want to.

(If you want to call the above paragraph just another "story," you can. But it may be as close as we can get to a basic understanding of what's really going on.)

The cosmos is awesome and infinite beyond all comprehension. A religion is a series of ideas and customs that exist in our minds at the cognitive level. Underneath those exist deeper perceptions that the

> *Super-subconsciously, we are* all INVOLUNTARY BELIEVERS.

religious ideas are based on, or rather, which cause the individual's religion or spiritual belief system to formulate itself in the first place, in response to those perceptions. These perceptions can be traced back to the core of our own being, to the core of reality itself, if we do so with enough desire for enlightenment and awareness of what is involved.

Even agnostics and atheists subconsciously buy into certain *basic ideas*[1] found in all the faiths. They have to, because they are also human and possess the capacity to indirectly perceive their own infinitude, and to be subconsciously frightened by it.

3 "Standard" Or "Basic" Theology

The concepts detailed below aren't really specific beliefs, but rather commonsense answers to universal questions that we all ask ourselves, whether we consciously want to or not.

- Who or what created everything? Where did it all come from? Something's responsible. We'll call it *God*.

- The world is often painful, and reliable sources of good sometimes become evil. The cause of this is complex. How do I personalize and make this problem easy to relate to? Well, we can think of it somehow as a mysterious, powerful living thing whose nature is to do evil things. Let's call it *the devil*.

> *Theoretical work in modern physics supports the idea that* EVERYTHING WE IMAGINE DOES, IN A SENSE, EXIST.

- I was a good person in spite of all my suffering in life. Isn't there a payoff somewhere? Yes—there must be a better place many of us go to; we'll call it *heaven*.

- Some people are primarily bad or evil, even though they may do well or seem happy. Where will they go? We'll use the word *hell*.

- Some people become inexplicably happier, or have undeserved luck out of the blue. There has to be some mysterious mechanism through which God affects their lives. We'll give it the term *grace*.

- Some people seem to become happier and more confident when they find religion, because they believe God will give them more fortunate circumstances in the afterlife. We'll call it *salvation*.

- The leaders of nations and armies misbehave; things always seem to be getting worse. But it's inconceivable that God would let his signature creature and civilization succumb completely to the devil. So just as he saves qualified individuals, he must save qualified groups and nations. The most natural way we can imagine him doing this—a way that we can relate to—is with special people doing great things in the world for God. We'll call them *prophets* and *messiahs*.

> *Salvation and enlightenment*
> *are TWO DIFFERENT THINGS.*

RAB'IA AL-BASRI—*8th Cent. Sufi ascetic poet-saint, Iraq. Most of what is known of her life is clouded in legend. Born into a poor family, she left home when a famine swept through her area, was caught while begging food, sold into slavery and later released by her master when he perceived her holiness. As a teacher, she refused many offers of marriage and was noted for her spontaneous devotional poetry, which others transcribed. Traditional likeness.*

- Since there was a beginning of time when God created the universe, there will also be an end. Because our souls are eternal, we are naturally concerned with what will happen to us at that time. We may as well call that the *Day of Judgment*.

(These beliefs occur in the Eastern faiths as well, although in a less obvious way. You have to dig further into the stories and commentaries to find them.)

4   Seeing Through Basic Theology

The central thing to appreciate is that all these notions are merely *logical inferences*—things people automatically figure out simply from the way reality is set up. We learn these and related terms while growing up, as part of our general vocabulary, whether or not we get any religions training. As nouns, these concepts are archetypal, existing at more profound levels within our minds than most things do, and corresponding to deeper, generic realities not apparent to the senses.[2]

> *We ALL have to organize the universe in our heads, BECAUSE WE ARE HUMAN.*

These ideas, therefore, are part of a vitally important, precognitive superstructure which maintains our perceived universe in basically the same way that six flat surfaces maintain the existence of a room.[3] We may not consciously think "God," "heaven" and so on are real, but subconsciously most of us have to, to some degree—unless we're ready for enlightenment. When that occurs, the external and internal attachments associated with *all* our ideas dissolve completely. The "six walls" vanish.

> *A finitely perceived universe cannot coexist in our minds with the INFINITUDE THAT REALLY IS.*

The more mature our thinking is, the less important these ideas (attachments) are, until they finally disappear completely with the cataclysmic understanding that we *are* God to begin with, and always were.

5   Literalist Thought Acknowledged

The structure of religion, of course, also includes literalist beliefs such as those examined in the preceding chapter. Appreciating the inevitability and importance of these beliefs helps us understand (be compassionate about) the problems they cause in the adult world.

In this book the term *religion* is generally equated with fundamentalist or literalist belief (Ch.2,S.4), because this type of belief most directly associates religion with concrete phenomena found in culture and history. In the early stages of human psychological development associated with children and young people, literalist belief is a natural

> *Parents who decry myths and fairy tales DO THEIR CHILDREN A REAL DISSERVICE.*

53

phase and cannot be avoided. In some cases, however, it persists all the way through an otherwise educated adult's life.[4] Until recently—the last century or so—this most simple type of belief is what the vast majority of followers subscribed to. Although college-level critical thinking has become widespread, substantial numbers of not-so-literal believers remain strongly sympathetic to parts of literal belief that many would find obviously questionable. I use the term *orthodox thought* to encompass this larger group of believers who continue to profess at least some of these dubious notions.

Religious scriptures don't fall out of the sky. We make gains in spirituality when we no longer "waffle" over implausible ideas, and become more certain of profound realities we don't so much understand as *feel*.

6   The Origin And Importance Of Myth

Myths are very important. They are "larger than life" ideas that, true or not, command belief on the part of many due to their luminosity.

Once you realize that NOTHING in a great myth is literally true, its SPIRITUAL BENEFIT multiplies with deeper RESONANCE IN YOUR PSYCHE.

How to understand this? First of all, God/Self, the Ultimate Reality, we can say has a "mind." This mind is energy—pure energy, perhaps, of the most subtle, refined, transcendent and powerful sort. This energy is beyond words to express, other than perhaps in the vaguest poetic terms: maybe it could be called "beauty." The mind of man, on the other hand, is usually confined to practical and rational thought, and occasional flights of fancy.

But there's a middle ground. God's energy pours out of the cosmos, as it were, and takes on different basic forms and aspects, crystallizing into created reality.[5] Within that, in the realm of human affairs, a range of basic objects and associated feelings come into being: "saint/love" would be one such object. Sinner/hatred, warrior/bravery, coward/timidity; king/charismatic, cripple/repulsive would be others, and so on.

Now, the most widespread form of human learning, even today overall, has always been narrative and story. Elders of societies made up the first stories—partially, no doubt, from their own dreams and visions. They and their descendants projected their own humanity onto the universe; peopling it with the same stock characters everywhere (such as those above), and naturally clothing those characters in cultural garb familiar to them. They related these stories to everyone else, and in this way understood the dramas and themes of life. Myths, so to speak, are therefore the *dreams of cultures;*[6] as such, they are naturally invested with the numinous energy of the divine template for whatever universal dilemma or situation they mean to illustrate. They represent a level of creation that has not yet descended to earth. When it does, different versions of the same myth naturally manifest in various cultures.

> *The NUMINOUS ENERGY of myths "possesses" many people powerfully enough for them to be GRANTED LITERAL BELIEF.*

> *WE NO LONGER BELIEVE MYTHS WHEN WE FIND similar levels of joy and wonder in the outside world.*

The thing to appreciate here is how natural it is that this occurs. As certain stories acquire more and more importance for certain cultures, divine/mythic energy enlivens them, just as salt dissolves into water until the water reaches its saturation point. Problems, of course, begin when modern followers don't realize that the true lessons of myths do not lie with literal interpretations of them.

7   Believing In Myths

Myths are powerful because they portray aspects of life and the human condition that we can already *find within ourselves*, even if we may only dimly recognize or understand them; and they represent qualities we are capable of *developing in ourselves*, however much we may think otherwise. People who do not understand this put themselves in a different category, and don't see themselves as capable of "participating" in the myth.

The myth did happen. It is real. But it represents a supernatural, Godly realm of inherently superior beings—different from life on earth. Ordinary people, naturally, cannot live up to this. So, in spite of its reality, the value of the myth can never be more than inspirational—it's not possible to have that same level of spirituality ourselves.

PADRE PIO—*Early/Mid 20th Cent. Catholic friar, Italy. He is noteworthy not only for experiencing the stigmata, but also for manifestation of abilities, powers, and tendencies more typically associated with eastern saints: bilocation, levitation, miraculous healings, and periods of extraordinary abstinence from sleep and nourishment. Never well enough documented to satisfy critics, worldwide reports of such phenomena lend them plausibility for believers.*

For most of these believers, this categorization and its attendant assumptions are subconscious. Also usually subconscious is the comparison they go on to make of themselves with the myth, as well as the verdict they come up with: *I am sinful and wretched.* All kinds of rationalized misbehaviors result from this, especially in some branches of Protestant Christianity, as anyone familiar with its history of scams and scandals can attest. (More on this in Appendix 3.) All this, of course, reinforces an even more deluded self-image among many followers of these groups. Similar dynamics exist among literalist and some orthodox followers of other faiths.

NAGA KANYA—*Hindu and Buddhist snake Goddess. Superficial meanings: guardian of treasures in underworld, bestower of rain, and archenemy of giant bird Garuda. Profound meaning: awakened spiritual energy inside a seeker, perhaps in its healing, nourishing aspect. Courtesy Exotic India.*

CHAPTER SIX

Choices: The Supreme Being

The concept of God/Self is the most basic place to start a spiritual inquiry. This is probably the most technical chapter in the book, and has two parts to it: exploring the various ideas about God which people tend to have, and then elucidating in basic terms the most profound and appealing of them. Coming to terms with the more subtle concepts connected with monistic and panentheistic understandings of God is an important part of the foundation that must be laid before enlightenment becomes possible for most seekers.

If you have difficulties with God at all—and most people who have issues with the religions do—then this material may also help you get a perspective on where you've been and where you are now. You may recognize beliefs which you held previously, or are currently wrestling with; and in that connection perhaps experience tension between what you were taught and what you are beginning to realize makes more sense. Appreciating the deeper truths connected with more profound understandings makes it more difficult to continue associating impermanent things that you were taught about God, with God/Self as it really is.

1   Basic Concepts

The terms below provide a bullet-point summary of the different ways people have of viewing God.

Monotheism	Henotheism	Humanism/Secularism
Pantheism	Monism/Panentheism	Supernaturalism
Deism #1	Polytheism #1	
Deism #2	Polytheism #2/Paganism	

Those with academic training in religion or philosophy may recognize this as a rather confused list. Some of these terms (monotheism, polytheism) are familiar to lay readers and have easily recognized popular definitions; others (monism, panentheism, pantheism, deism, henotheism), are more technical terms in philosophy of religion, and not as well known. Humanism and supernaturalism don't focus on God, but they are both common world-views involving or implying things about God, so they are of interest.

> *At SOME level, everyone possesses an OBJECTIVE DESCRIPTION of ultimate reality, as THEY UNDERSTAND IT.*

2 "Historical Development" And Rising Consciousness

I put this title in quotes to indicate that the historical information briefly presented below is not of central importance. It may be helpful, however, to see how all these concepts relate to each other.

It is crucial to appreciate that, except for deism #2, which involves science, these different concepts of God have *always existed* in different people's heads, even if they didn't have the vocabulary to express them. We

> *These ideas represent the NATURAL VARIETY OF WAYS that people HAVE ALWAYS HAD of understanding and relating to God, or ultimate concern.*

all know what it's like to feel or understand something that we don't know how to say. The paragraph below links these ideas together and explains the rising prominence of panentheism and monism.

It makes sense that, as our intelligence evolved in prehistoric times, we first peopled the universe with our projections, first with various small spirits and powers (polytheism II). Those spirits and powers may have been at first implicitly understood as expressions or "parts" of some underlying power that runs through everything (pantheism). And some people were mainly interested in occult powers and forces (supernaturalism). This basically corresponds to the earliest forms of indigenous religion, and was prevalent over most of the planet in ancient times. Later—as

> DO YOU BELIEVE *in ghosts or spirits? Is IT REALLY SURPRISING that the ancients would people the entire universe with deities?*

rituals and oral traditions developed around major projections—more elaborate deities came into being which were thought to represent aspects or powers of an all-embracing impersonal principle (polytheism I). Individual worshippers, seeking a sense of unity, subsequently tended to attribute all powers and abilities to their favorite deity (henotheism), just as devotees did to their only deity (monotheism) in systems that discouraged polytheism. All this gradually displaced or absorbed most indigenous traditions as civilizations developed. As this happened, there were always small numbers of people who understood God as both creating the universe and being its manifestation (panentheism and monism), but because this requires a high level of interest and a subtle intellect, the natural tendency among monotheists especially was to think of God as being "up there" and separate from what he/she/it created (deism I). The advent and development of science led some to believe that a cosmic intelligence embodying all the laws of nature is what constitutes God (deism II). Deism I (Judaism, Christianity and Islam) went on to become the most prevalent form of religion and is still growing. But as science continued to disaffect people from religion, the idea became more prominent among many that all powers and potential goodness lay within man (humanism). Finally, some people don't relate to God *per se*, but continue to be interested in esoteric and occult things that at least associate them with divine power (again, supernaturalism).

> WITHOUT *a subtle intellect, there's a natural tendency to think of God as being "up there," EXISTING SEPARATELY FROM CREATION.*

The summary above treats most of these terms in a vague and sometimes inaccurate way.[1] We need a better sense of what each of them means to see whether, and to what degree, we can subscribe to them.

3   Belief Systems Involving An Ultimate Reality

Monotheism—Umbrella term for belief in only one God, who is usually thought of as being apart from the universe he created. It is both personal and masculine in character. *Note:*

> *Behind the scenes, western thinkers DEVELOPED THE FEMININE ASPECT of god as well.*

In the general sense, monotheism is the perhaps the most commonsensical and appealing view, involving both God's oneness in everything, and also his transcendence beyond everything. Not surprisingly, this is the way most people everywhere speak about God in informal conversation. Also, while on the social and political level this deity is thought of only as transcendent, the deeper philosophies of the monotheistic faiths all develop the panentheistic aspects of this one God as well.

ALAN WATTS—20th Cent. British Episcopal priest turned radio show host, maverick philosophy professor and Zen teacher in the US. He believed in "divine madness" in personal relationships, experimented with psychedelics and was an active figure in human potential movement; and probably did more than anyone else to introduce Zen Buddhism to the Western world.

Pantheism—Belief that God exists as an impersonal force or entity that pervades the entire universe. *Note:* The often-heard academic definition of 'God being identical with the physical universe' is misleading, since it renders God superfluous. As human beings, people project or overlay some subtle conception of God *onto* the universe; pantheists just favor more impersonal conceptions ("cosmic energy" or "great spirit") since they tend to be nature-lovers. A personal relationship is often claimed, however.

Deism #1—Belief that God exists apart from the universe that he created. *Note:* This is the general superficial idea that many monotheistic believers have of God from having attending Sunday school, or from reading certain parts of their scriptures. This deity sometimes interferes with the universe through acts of "supernatural intervention." It's important to realize that praying to a deistic God can only help you so much, since he exists apart from the universe and therefore cannot really "be there" for you completely.

Given that supernatural events are SO COMMON (if you count cases of intuitive knowledge), the deistic God MAKES NO SENSE AT ALL.

Deism #2—Belief that God exists, in some personal way, as the source and sum total of all the laws of nature.[2] *Note:* Although for some people, the personal aspect of this God renders it contradictory to inflexible law and therefore untenable, others find a powerful personal element in the "romance of science"[3]—a sense of reverence and awe connected with the grand architecture of the universe.

Henotheism—Belief that a single deity in a polytheistic system can do anything for its followers, even though only some powers are traditionally attributed to that deity. *Note:* This is not really a theory concerning the nature of God, but an important understanding of how human psychology instinctively begins to understand the oneness of God, even if other deities are acknowledged. This dynamic is universal, taking a different form in Western systems. Some Catholics, for example, devote almost all their worship and veneration to the Madonna or one of the patron saints, effectively attributing all powers to them, even though God and Christ are technically of greater importance.

Because they are human, even the hardest-nosed scientists and most inhuman killers possess a MEANINGFUL (TOUCHY-FEELY) RELATIONSHIP WITH GOD at some level.

Panentheism—Belief that God is both identical with the universe in that he underlies and pervades everything, and greater than the universe since he also creates and maintains it. *Note:* This is the term in western philosophy of religion which combines God's two major aspects into a single paradox: immanent *and* tran-scendent, in the world *but* not of

"Graven images" often DO US THE SERVICE of portraying SENSUAL REALITIES, which we must EMBRACE AND INTEGRATE.

it, etc. The main difference between it and monism is that panenthe-ism speaks of these two aspects as sort of coexisting, instead of being (mysteriously and incomprehensively) identical. The panentheistic deity's "center" is everywhere.[4]

Monism—Belief in a single, unifying principle that encompasses everything, and which ultimately does not exist apart from the believer. *Note:* In mysticism, this term is often used to refer to a "heart" or "common core" which all religions are said to share at the deepest level. Capitalized words such as "Source," "Truth," or "the Absolute" are used to refer to it in a more impersonal way.

Polytheism #1—Belief in the existence of a number of major and often minor deities, together with a single underlying reality (often mythologized as a high god) that they all spring from. Note: This is

(On the THEORETICAL level, MARXISM is one of the most BEAUTIFUL AND COMPASSIONATE secular philosophies ever devised.)

often thought of as compatible with monism and panentheism, since the latter two also postulate an ultimate reality that naturally expresses itself as various powers and forces. The major Eastern faiths, actually (Hinduism, Buddhism and Taoism)—or rather, the individual follower's version of

whichever one he follows—can be either monistic, monotheistic *or* polytheistic, depending on which aspect he or she relates to most strongly.

4   Belief Systems Not Focusing On An Explicit Ulitmate Reality

Polytheism #2 or Paganism—Belief in the existence of a number of "spiritual" or in some sense disembodied entities, or forces. *Note:* Whereas polytheism I refer to an organized system of distinct deities with an ultimate reality underlying it; polytheism II and paganism refer to belief in more loosely defined spirits of whatever sort, with only an implicit concept of an ultimate reality, often not expressed in the culture's language.

Humanism or Secularism—Belief in the idea that all "spiritual" fulfillment stems from the potential found in human beings for love, compassion, justice, and so on. There are humanist versions of belief in God, but his role would seem to be secondary. The emphasis is on practical concern with this world, rather than preoccupation with higher realities. *Note:* Insofar as people believe in "themselves," humanism or secularism more broadly understood encompasses anyone's understanding of his or her highest potential and ultimate concern. *Hedonism*, for example, is a type of secularism. Rather than valuing religion, its followers hold their own ideas about how human potential gets its greatest expression and fulfillment through the pursuit of pleasure. *Empiricism* would be another type of humanism, finding its fulfillment in the romance of science mentioned above. As far as God is concerned, at best these are agnostic perspectives, thinking of him, again, perhaps as a Freudian patriarchal projection[5] or something of that sort.

GAZING UP AT OUR PARENTS when we were six months old–for Freudians, these mythically giant figures BECOME GODS LATER ON.

Supernaturalism—Spirituality in the form of preoccupation with various kinds of powers or higher forces, with questions concerning God of secondary importance. *Note:* What all these preoccupations have in common is that they at least associate[6] the believer with a transcendent power or entity. Examples would be interest in spiritual or psychic powers such as telepathy or astral projection, higher beings such as angels or disembodied masters, UFOs and/or theories of ancient extraterrestrial visitation, the glories of Atlantis and the like. These seekers may believe in God, but they tend to equate divine power with whatever occult or esoteric phenomenon preoccupies them.

5 Your Path And Concept Of God

As you study the more mystical ideas of God in the different faiths, you begin to realize that there are basic common dimensions of understanding and relating to God which different parts of all the religions share. There is a monotheistic *aspect* to all the Eastern faiths insofar as some of their sects focus on a

> ORTHODOX MUSLIMS *try not to "WORSHIP SKELETONS," but often find themselves involved in popular piety surrounding* LOCAL SUFI PATRON SAINTS.

single deity to the exclusion of all others, and there are polytheistic or even paganistic *aspects* to all the Western faiths, insofar as they value pilgrimage sites, deceased patron saints, and living masters, to say nothing of the indigenous folk practices which they often embrace. Understandings like these help us perceive "the transcendent unity of religions"[7] for ourselves.

JESUS CHRIST—*1ˢᵗ Cent. Pharisee Jew, Palestine. His life and teachings provided inspiration for the development of Christianity. Mainstream scholars regard his immediate and spectacular miracles (water into wine, etc.) as embellishments for the sake of clarity and easy understanding. A number of non-biblical ancient references to Christ establish that he did exist. Traditional depiction.*

Especially in America and Europe, for decades now most of the religions have been steadily losing followers, and as affluence, science and technology establish themselves in the developing world, the faiths currently gaining followers in those countries will likely start losing them as well. Moreover, with increasing cross-cultural awareness, more and more people are most comfortable with a combination of influences

> *It would seem that* COMMITMENT TO PRACTICES *is important, not to a religion.*

from both eastern and western faiths, as well as with comparable secular influences in meaning and ultimate concern.

It's actually advantageous that this picture is so confusing: fewer people than ever end up getting trained in literalist beliefs, and more people than ever are forced to confront mystical perspectives. As a result, the value of "commitment" to a spiritual path will likely be understood more generically. What's not always easy is discerning what balance of different influences is right for you. Again, this book's thesis is the idea that, through whatever combination of practices, everyone sooner or later comes around to a panentheistic or monistic orientation.[8]

WINGED HEART—*Sufi symbol. Superficial meaning: none. Profound meaning: Heart ascending to God/Self; crescent reflecting more and more light from within until it merges. Courtesy Wikimedia Commons.*

CHAPTER SEVEN

Choices: Afterlife and Cosmology

Central to people's understandings of how the universe works spiritually is our knowledge concerning what happens after we die. A better understanding of the mechanics and explanatory power of the different scenarios involved is helpful, since it points to the greater plausibility of the monistic view.

Although they are generally scattered throughout their works, taken together a significant corpus of material from renowned spiritual teachers, philosophers and mediums exists on the topic of the afterlife.[1] While not reviewing or even summarizing these sources, this chapter does present some main understandings from orthodox and mystical religious traditions, which do mirror in general terms much of what these sources have written.

1 Understanding The Scenarios

There are basically five models or scenarios reviewed in this chapter, most of which have many variations. A profusion of often-repetitive detail exists in world literature about each of these from all major religious and mystical traditions. However, not much detail is necessary to get a sense of the important differences between each of these models. Here we will see what they have to say about only the most basic and important questions people have. These are taken to be 1) *in what state or manner will I exist after I die?* 2) *If my conduct or behavior in this life is judged or assessed in some way, how does that happen and what transpires as a result?* And finally 3) *what part does God play in all this, and how does he go about it?*

I've tried to develop these models further, filling in plausible detail for the sake of MORE COMPLETE ANSWERS FOR SOPHISTICATED SEEKERS.

For the most part these questions are answered in only a vague and general way by clergy in the world's faiths, again because ordinary religious teaching is meant for popular consumption. I've done my best to give each system a greater level of detail. Of course the greater, overarching reason why these scenarios often do not answer our questions sufficiently is because we are all unique. *Each of us is, paradoxically, the being and source of our entire afterlife experience, in the same way that we are each the being and source of the entire universe in our capacity for enlightenment.* In the process of getting there, however, there are obviously many similarities between most people's experiences, so a study of these scenarios can be fruitful.

2   Orthodox Verses Mystical Views

The most essential thing to bear in mind as you look through these paradigms is that religious cosmologies can be interpreted at two levels. First is the conventional or orthodox level taught by the religions, meant for anyone to be able to learn. These are dualistic and assume that space and time go on forever, and that God does his work within that framework. The second is the mystical level, which is monistic, paradoxical, and assumes that God creates space and time just like he does everything within and beyond it (higher dimensions, etc.).

A closer look at this space-and-time issue illustrates this difference. What happens *before* creation, and *after* the Day of Judgment? In the orthodox heaven-and-hell (H&H) scenario, God does all his creating

At the orthodox level, Western cosmologies see creation as a one-time event, with nothing before or after. Eastern systems see it as ENDLESSLY REPEATING CYCLES OF MANIFESTATION.

> CONSISTENT THEMES IN SPIRITUAL PHILOSOPHY LIKEN DEATH TO A LONG SLEEP, *with a semblance of our body existing after death just as it does in dreams.*

and judging at the beginning and ending, respectively, of that time interval. What happens before or after this creation time-interval is unaccounted for. In mystical interpretations of this system, on the other hand, Eastern and Western thought becomes essentially identical. At this level, space and time are part of what God creates, so it's not possible for there to be any questions involving time outside of that creation.

And so, Western and Eastern mystical doctrines, at least in spirit, have similarly profound levels of deeper interpretation. An intellectual tension exists between orthodox understandings which leave questions unanswered, and mystical understandings which "answer" all of them.

The state of our existence in the afterlife is one thing that can be clarified briefly before getting into the five models. Especially at the orthodox level, except for Judaism the world's faiths are almost universal in teaching that we do have a body in the afterlife. The physical body of course decays, but we retain a spiritual one, which is usually thought of as resembling our old body and occupying the same space, although not in the same way (Ch.9,S.3).

Other relevant information is discussed below in connection with each model.

3 Spirit Worlds System (SW)

These systems are found in indigenous traditions. This scenario postulates a high god who created everything at some point in the past, but who is distant, and typically plays no part in everyday worship and belief. People's souls go to the "spirit world," which to some extent mirrors the world in real life, and provides ways (through shamans, etc.) for the deceased to resolve issues through interaction with the living. There is a tendency for the dead to "hang

> *You could say orthodox cosmologies are* WRITTEN BY SPIN DOCTORS: *they* PROVIDE CONVENIENT EXPLANATIONS *for those who don't care to think.*

around" his or her home environs and/or the place of death for a while. Sometimes an "underworld" or other realms of pain and suffering exist separately from more typical spirit realms, where certain animals and bad or unfortunate people go.[2] In the most developed systems, entire spiritual universes are thought to exist which parallel this one.[3] Often, long-deceased relatives more than five or six generations back seem to no longer exist after a while, perhaps inhabiting planes of existence somehow more distant than the immediate spirit worlds where the more recently deceased go, if not merging with the general energy of God (after perhaps having cleared up all their issues[4]). Even so, prominent ancestors are often worshipped, and typically function as intermediaries between living humans and important deities that often exist within such systems. In contrast to the Heaven and

Go into a family's home, and look for the cluster of pictures together in a special corner somewhere. WHO ARE THOSE PICTURES OF?

Hell concepts of the major faiths, again most of these spirit worlds are usually thought of as being more local, or "closer" in some sense to where the deceased person lived. God, or spirit, is understood in two contexts: either as a vaguely pantheistic sense of energy that is everywhere, or as one of the major deities or spirits in the system. Unless you are one of the rare, historically important personages in the culture who ends up getting deified, the concept of enlightenment doesn't really occur in these systems, unless implicitly as an eventual merging of the soul back into the pantheistic background as mentioned.

JAMAT ALI—*19th/20th Cent. Sufi Pir, Punjab, India, and Pakistan. Ali represents a tendency sometimes seen especially in Hindu saints: to sit in meditation for so long and often that their limbs atrophy or, as in Ali's case, their eyes grow intolerant to a normal amount of light. Toward the latter part of his life, his followers would bring him out of his hut once a year for musical performances and other ceremonies.*

The Hindu idea that you can only make spiritual progress while in human form on earth DOES NOT SEEM TO HOLD WATER.

Discussion. The great merit of these systems is that they are commonsensical and intuitive, operating according to the feelings and attachments of people who have not, in a sense, been "corrupted" by science and psychological theory. Historically, as civilizations developed and more sophisticated cosmologies were devised in connection with the major religions, spirit world paradigms like this ended up being embraced by those major faiths, becoming the "folk religion" aspect or that religion, usually practiced by less educated people living in rural areas. In and of themselves, spirit world systems certainly answer more questions than the larger heaven and hell systems which end up encompassing them—at least as those heaven and hell systems are taught to the orthodox faithful. When they get incorporated into these larger cosmologies, the spirit worlds that persons enter immediately after death are often thought of as stopovers, or way stations, which souls inhabit for a short time before moving on to higher realms connected with a major or monotheistic deity of the major religion.

4   Heaven And Hell System (H&H)

These are found in the Abrahamic (Western) religions. This worldview postulates at least three separate realities that God creates when he brings the universe into being: heaven, hell and Earth. According to what we deserve, we go to a better or worse place than Earth after death. The varieties of this belief primarily involve whether or not there are different levels of heaven and hell and, if so, how many there are and whether or not we stay forever where we are first sent. Most declare that we can move from one realm to another. If both are in store for us, hell is visited first where purification takes place. Again, different levels of hell are implied, and some can

In orthodox systems enlightenment doesn't exist, since you ONLY END UP BEING "WITH" GOD INSTEAD OF BECOMING HIM.

suffer eternal damnation. In some systems, purification happens in a place that is thought to exist apart from heaven and hell, therefore making up a four-part universe.[5] (This fourth realm is an important idea if there is thought to be only a single heaven and a single hell, otherwise still-imperfect souls who potentially qualify for heaven would have no place in which to resolve their remaining issues. This fourth realm is a superfluous idea if there is more than one level of heaven and hell, since it could be construed as a light-duty level of hell.) Also, some say that we can move through successively higher levels of heaven, to be "closer to" God than we would be if we merely "went to heaven."[6] In either case, we have "eternal life"

> *Popular liberal sermons understand heaven and hell to be states of mind, which* EFFECTIVELY MERGES THEM WITH EASTERN DOCTRINE.

even though, according to this model, God creates the soul at conception. This means that the soul is not eternal after all, unless it is exists as a kind of separate potential within God before it gets created.[7] Things happen the way they do due to the will of God through his created laws of nature, which he sometimes interrupts through supernatural intervention, in which those laws are overridden with a different version of God's will for some period of time. God exists as the Deism #1 scenario (Ch. 4). Finally, the universe as we know it comes to an end on the Day of Judgment, when everyone has either eternal life in heaven or (in some versions) stays in hell forever. Evil is understood primarily as disobedience. In orthodox versions, enlightenment doesn't exist in these systems, since in heaven the deceased person is ultimately only "with" God, however close he or she may get to him. But this is patently false for some of the mystics in these traditions. There is no doubt that many of them believed and experienced that it is possible to eventually merge with God and exist *as* Him/Her/It.[8]

> *How can a soul be eternally damned* IF GOD CREATED IT?

Discussion. The way the H&H system is usually presented involves obvious contradictions and many questions that are either unanswered or answered too vaguely. Is the soul eternal or not? Does achieving the highest heaven, or does just going to a single one represent the greatest possible human fulfillment? Why is there the particular number of heavens and hells that there are? Is there nothing at all before creation and after the Day of Judgment? How can a soul be eternally damned if God created it? And so on. On the positive side, when interpreted with more liberal detail, these systems acquire features in common with some SW scenarios. Both have a number of planes of post-mortem existence and ethical qualifications for moving between them (although in the SW scenario these are only implied, and not written down). In popular sermons of liberal denominations, finally, heaven and hell are spoken of not so much as places as they are states of mind that we create for ourselves in this world. This effectively merges Abrahamic understandings of these places with those of Eastern mystics.

5 Karma And Reincarnation System (K&R)

Belief that the soul transmigrates from the deceased body to a new one, and experiences in subsequent incarnations consequences of acts committed in previous ones. Varieties of this belief include whether or not under certain conditions humans can reincarnate into animal forms or vice-versa, whether or not spiritual progress can be made in the afterlife, how long and where one might spend time on a higher plane between incarnations and what determines this interval, and if an evolutionary ladder of progressively more complex organisms is involved which souls transmigrate up through. In this system, creation is inherent in God's nature; he creates the universe out of himself, producing, as it were, a stage or drama in which all creatures continually reincarnate and eventually realize that the point of life is to find their way back and reunite with their source. Realization of God/Self is a human birthright, "pulling" all sentient beings back to itself sooner or later. Creation "never happened" precisely because it is ongoing and eternal, brimming and overflowing

> *Astrophysicists' Anthropic Hypotheses, and their discovery that we are at the "center" of an expanding universe, are JUST MORE EXPRESSIONS OF MYSTICAL PARADOX.*

with inexhaustible potential; and nothing is saved or damned because everything good and evil (understood as ignorance rather than disobedience) exists in the first place as a spectrum (Ch.2,S.5-6), constituting merely the variety of creation, and not any valuation of what is in it.[9]

> *One of the appeals of the K&R system over the H&H system is that, although grace is operative in both, THE K&R SYSTEM IS MORE DETERMINISTIC.*

Discussion. As a belief, reincarnation is based on the observation that all created things, without exception, move through a basic cycle of creation or manifestation, followed eventually by dissolution or transformation, only to give rise to more creation. Most objects in the universe "repeat themselves" (Ch.4,S.2); those that don't repeat themselves come from recycled constitutive elements and compounds of previous objects, and merely take new shapes. This provides what many consider to be satisfactory resolutions, although in very general terms, to most of the issues mentioned in the H&H and SW systems. One of the appeals of the K&R system over the H&H system is that, although grace is operative in both, the K&R system is more deterministic. When a soul leaves a body at death, it takes with it a record of all its *karma*—the yet unfulfilled consequences of the thoughts and actions the person performed in his/her last as well as previous lifetimes. Based on that template, the soul enters an afterlife which to some extent is unique to it, and later in its journey God/Self *configures*, so to speak, an appropriate subsequent reality for the person to be reborn into, in order to undergo those consequences and make new choices to perhaps bring him-/herself closer to enlightenment. As far as problems go, one issue with the spiritual-ladder and reincarnation-between-species version of this scenario is the disparity between the larger numbers of lower organisms, and the much fewer higher ones they would have to reincarnate up into. A conglomerating effect is sometimes proposed to account for this, in which many souls merge together into larger ones.

> *THERE IS NO ABSOLUTE CERTAINTY AROUND "THE WORD OF GOD": enlightenment can't be measured and mediums can't be double-checked.*

SHANKARACHARYA— 8ᵀᴴ Cent. Hindu monastic and commentator; formulated the Advaita Vedanta philosophy. He started four important monasteries and ten orders of swamis (monks) in India. The story goes that his mother refused him permission at age 8 to take monastic vows, but finally relented when a crocodile seized his foot and seemed intent on devouring him—until permission was given. Deified later by some groups, high-ranking Shaivite Hindu clerics bear Shankara's name as part of their title. Likeness from statue.

6   Quantum Re-Expression System (QR)

This is basically a "scientized" version of the K&R system, appealing to more agnostic thinkers. The subtle elements or life force of the body are thought to somehow merge, blend or are reabsorbed back into a kind of subtle matrix or source that underlies space/time, and which,

> *This system subscribes to* ALL THE INSIGHTS CONNECTED WITH MODERN PHYSICS *insofar as they relate to human perception and consciousness.*

at least in theory, operates according to complex and as–yet–unknown laws of physics. With the absorption of such energies, this source continually re-expresses itself with new manifestations into space and time. Good and evil are understood as degrees of harmony and disharmony, which again balance out and follow each other according to deeds performed. Varieties of this belief involve different proposed mechanisms and laws by which this subtle matrix might operate.

> IF WE LEAVE MATTER BEHIND *and transfer our souls into computers, will they* be MORE SPIRITUAL?

Discussion. Quantum Re-expression is the name I give to this "New Age" way of thinking about reality, in which religious and spiritual questions are often understood scientifically, and/or are thought to be amenable to technological intervention through neurochemistry, cybernetics, and so on. It subscribes to all the insights connected with modern physics (Ch.1,S.4) insofar as they relate to human perception and consciousness. Some say this system can eventually answer *all* questions, not only because of its cyclical nature and determinism, but also because the spiritual laws responsible for miracles in this world (the grace of God itself) can one day be understood and even applied through mechanisms that operate at higher levels of reality.[10] For some, a primary objection to this system is that it is fundamentally impersonal. It just "is," and doesn't require any special or divine forces to operate. Others do find a personal dimension. A deeper objection to this system is that, for many, it represents the age-old, delusional *hubris* of mankind, harkening back to the Tower of Babel allegory in the Old Testament, in which God was forced to sabotage our prideful efforts to reach him and master all his powers.

7   No Afterlife (Strict Empiricism)

Belief that the body simply decays and that concepts such as God, soul, etc. do not refer to anything actually existing in the universe (Ch.6,S.4). Like all other thoughts and mental experiences—whether referring to real things or not—the concept "God" is thought to be only a by-product of subtle and complex neurochemistry. The "higher" planes of reality implied by quantum physics may indeed have objective existence of some kind, but they don't originate from our own being in the way that the larger universe metaphysically originates from each of us in the monistic view.

While important on the planetary scale, for many people social media has been SPIRITUALLY DISASTROUS.

Nonbelievers can also attain enlightenment, because as human beings they are ALSO SUBJECT TO DISILLUSIONMENT AND DESPAIR.

Discussion. This scenario is a variety of humanism; I include it on its own because, although held by less than 10% of people

worldwide, it is prominent among intelligentsia and is indirectly pro-
moted by all areas of technological development. Like the SW an
H&H systems, it is dualistic; as such, its world-view paradigm is that
of classical physics ("atoms in the void"[11]), which is fatalistic and leaves
no room for any kind of divine intervention. Nothing is understood as
fundamentally transcendent or eternal, since everything, including the
paranormal occurrences associated with modern physics, can eventually be understood through laws of nature yet undiscovered. In these
seekers, spirituality expresses itself through the degree of conviction,
enthusiasm and wonder they have for the human enterprise and their
participation in it. Although rare, ordinary work carried out with sufficient dedication and focus can have the same purifying effect within
empiricist beliefs as spiritual practices have in mystical traditions, and
can also result in enlightenment, even with no involvement in religion
or performance of spiritual practice[12].

PART 3

THE MECHANICS OF SPIRITUALITY

In this last part we concern ourselves with what people actually do to pursue mystically-oriented spirituality: the various practices there are, the different attitudes and orientations we can have in doing them, the now-worldwide phenomenon of yoga in most all the faiths, the spiritual understanding of the human body and the energy that comes with it, the issue of interacting with God in a meaningful way, and teachers and groups.

Because the mystical orientation is fundamentally individual, I don't discuss groups in much detail. Groups usually mirror the preferences and backgrounds of the people who start them, so the teachers themselves are given more attention.

AHIMSA HAND—*symbol of the Jain religion. The hand is in abaya mudra (blessings, fearlessness). The circle and spokes represent samsara (wheel of life) and reincarnation. The Sanskrit ahimsa is in the center, meaning nonviolence. Courtesy Wikimedia Commons.*

CHAPTER EIGHT

Spiritual Practices

Religions do not have different practices. They all have the same practices clothed in different languages, customs, and degrees of emphasis. Understanding the rough universality of the practice categories discussed in this chapter is part of realizing that none of us are truly special or different.

Many seekers do practices because they know the world is transient, and that it's possible to get closer to God, if not merge with him. Spiritual practices draw grace and transform our inner being. They tend to be easier with groups and in spiritual settings, but as time goes on we become less and less dependent on people and places.

What methods should you use? The main factor is what works for you. Of course, the practices you do might dry up after a while, and you may battle with boredom and restlessness. And changing your practices raises a dilemma: there are benefits associate with austerity and commitment (Ch.6,S.5) as well as with change and flexibility. It depends on your situation and what you (and perhaps others) think is best for you.

If you're bored with everything, check in with yourself about convictions, priorities and attitude. Isn't God/Self out there somewhere, and shouldn't you have enough interest to do practices? In modern psychology, words like "should" or "must" are suspect, yet there is a sense of obligation in a conscious spiritual journey.

Most of the headings below are specific practices, but some are better described as attitudes or orientations. What most of them have

> *There will be inner obstacles; you can't always EXPECT TO ENJOY YOUR PRACTICES.*

in common is an effort to focus the mind, usually in a gentle way, with a sense of surrender and longing for grace underneath. Sometimes a distinction is made between orthodox or conventional practices, versus mystical practices—the major difference being that the latter are done for longer periods of time, and often with greater intensity. Ultimately this is misleading, however, since one blends into the other.

1   Devotions: An Initial Perspective From Organized Religion

This term is sometimes applied to basic practices performed in a more or less social context. Devotions include going to services, listening to sermons, basic rituals, giving to charity, attending celebrations and festivals, as well as basic respect for one's health and upkeep. (The last two of these are mentioned in very few front-

> *THIS FOUNDATION is necessary for a maturity BEYOND the normal sense of the word.*

line scriptures, but they are clearly implied by them.) These practices have always been thought valuable by spiritual teachers for cultivating the basic dimensions of a good morality. Of course, many of us get that not through religion at all, but as a result of good parenting.

More is said about some of these devotions below, since the spiritual dynamics behind some of them are important to understand.

2   Verbal And Silent Prayer

Whether out loud or silent, verbal prayer takes place on the cognitive level. Usually it expresses gratitude, adoration or submission, but may also include a request (Ch.11,S.6-9). When the worshipper no longer says anything even to him or herself, silent prayer commences, in which the person rests content with eyes closed.

Prayer is typically engaged in for short periods of time, such as one or two minutes. Many people pray (or do any spiritual practice) only during difficult periods of their lives. At the other extreme, many mystics pray throughout the day—that is, whenever they are not mentally engaged in something they have to do. They never ask for anything because all they want is to be closer to or united with God, and they don't know what that will involve at any given point in time.

A MAJOR DISCIPLINE-AVOIDANCE STRATEGY is to say that you talk to God all day long, whenever you feel like it.

As the most basic spiritual practice, prayer is, arguably, a universal human need. It is worth noting that even atheists (Ch.2), in moments of extreme danger or astonishment, will make exclamatory references such as *Oh my God!* with all the focus they can muster. (This is *not* just an expression in our language. People in all cultures naturally make exclamatory reference to "the Almighty" in those kinds of situations.)

3 Meditation

Although it has long been divorced from religion in the popular mind (for atheists interested stress reduction, it is divorced even from spirituality), meditation is the best-known mystical practice. It's appropriate to devote a fair amount of space to understanding it.

In the popular media, meditation often means to think about or ponder something in a subtle way. That's not how mystics understand it. Meditation, in all of the varied methods used to go about it, is basically a deepening of prayer, although in most cases the practitioner doesn't think of it that way. When prayer ceases to have words or cognitive content—when the experience of prayer focuses entirely on a subtle joy and tranquility inside one's self, *and* the person begins using some method to deepen it—meditation proper may be said to have begun. It is usually done for longer periods than prayer, ten minutes or more. An hour is not uncommon.

To the extent that the mind is agitated, and our health is affected by emotional issues, meditation has a LONG-TERM HARMONIZING EFFECT.

> *An enlightened person NEVER EXPERIENCES BOREDOM, even if he or she says they do.*

The object of meditation is to gradually tap into that aspect of our being which is already enlightened, and to use that power to purify and harmonize "the rest of us" in the subtle depths of the psyche. It does this both through grace, and our own self-effort (the "two wings" of the spiritual path).[1]

ANANDAMAYI MA—*Married but celibate ascetic (d. 1982), India. She seems to have had no teacher, and showed signs of unusual meditative detachment as a child. Although perhaps the most renowned 20th cent. female saint from the subcontinent, she possessed one "fanatical" idiosyncrasy: whenever her husband attempted sexual advances, her body would apparently go cold, "exhibiting signs of death."*

Especially if it is learned and practiced under good conditions, people commonly notice an immediate improvement in stress level, mental clarity, and overall well being. If psychological issues need to be resolved, meditating will cause the person to want to overcome them. Eventually, an "inner sweetness" is accessed and becomes an ongoing part of one's life.

Seekers at these levels of spirituality rarely, if ever, experience boredom, although as human beings it may seem like it. Even if such a person is stranded, unable to do anything for days on end except wait, there is a continual source of profound, integrated and effervescent joy they're always in touch with.

There are three reasons meditation can stop working, or "dry up" and yield no inner fruit even

> ONCE YOU GET A FIRM SENSE OF WHAT ENLIGHTENMENT IS, *nothing ever quite satisfies you again until you get there.*

after years of practice. The most common has to do with therapeutic issues that need to be addressed on the psychological level. Like anyone else, seekers sometimes ignore their personal issues (Ch.3,S.8) or don't recognize their severity. Beyond a certain point, the individual cannot advance further without addressing them. The second reason meditation can stop working relates to the person's health or environment. Physical pain, weakness, cold and fatigue can all interfere. Psychoactive drugs can also fog the mind too much for effective practice (although see S.14).

The third and most profound reason for this relates to what was said earlier about being "lost" (Ch.3,S.2). This can evolve into the classic "dark night of the soul," usually coming on gradually and resulting from all our comforting ideas about life, God, and spirituality being relentlessly stripped away. Many of us are raised with pleasant notions about these things which are either false or were never fully understood. Seekers are often left with a mild sense of despair, of not knowing anything after all. What is often not recognized about this "dark night" is that it's sometimes simply a matter of time. The understanding a person has gained needs to integrate into his or her life for a while. This process can't be rushed any more than the petals of a budding flower can be pried off without damaging the plant.

For the agnostically inclined, FOLLOWING ONE'S BREATHING is the most common technique.

The thing that best jump-starts meditation is *spiritual initiation* of some kind, which these days is easily done and takes a variety of forms, often without the sense of commitment that is traditionally required (Ch.10,S.5,7,and 8). More is said about meditation in Appendix 2.

4   Recollection

Basically this is meditation in everyday life. It refers to the practice of remembering God not cognitively (although a cognitive device is often used to do it), but by feeling his presence in your daily life when your mind is free and you're not thinking about anything in particular. Most seekers use the same device they use for meditation,

> *Inasmuch as it is nonverbal and we need exercise, getting "in the zone" with any activity* CAN BE THOUGHT OF AS VALID RECOLLECTION.

but of course in a less focused way since you're moving about and doing things. In some traditions, longer phrases or *mantras* (App.2) are used, and cognitive elements get involved in what amounts to continual prayer, rather than recollection. For the agnostically inclined, following one's breathing (most typically associated with Buddhism) is perhaps the most common technique.

Most mystics in the religions use rosaries of one sort or another. The object of this is not just to have a physical reminder of your interior practice, but also to embody and make it a more tangible experience.

5 Contemplation

This term is used in many ways; here we will define it as pondering something in a subtle way in order to better understand it, with divine assistance. Since thinking is involved, the thing to be better understood cannot, by

> *You gradually realize you possess an inner faculty* WHICH WILL RESPOND IF THE ISSUE IS TRULY IMPORTANT.

definition be the *essence* of God—at that point, you would be doing recollection (see above). A well-known general method of contemplation is described later in connection with the material about affirmations (Ch.11,S.9-10).

We can think of the practices described so far as a kind of continuum: verbal prayer being the shallowest, usually done formulaically and without thinking; recollection, which facilitates focused thinking during the day; contemplation to gain subtle understanding of something; and finally sitting meditation to contact levels deeper than the mind altogether.

The "answer" to whatever you're contemplating will come, but generally not in the way you might expect. This is described later in connection with more detailed instructions for contemplation (Ch.11,S.10). For some people, this faculty of "inner wisdom" manifests as an entity of some sort in dreams, such as an angel or guru whose teachings they follow.

6   Self-Inquiry

In the psychological context, self-in-quiry[2] refers simply to thinking through why we do what we do, usually in order to wrestle with our issues and improve our own behavior. Spiritually, it refers to progressively

> *ALL OTHER SPIRITUAL PRACTICES amount to self-inquiry under another name.*

discerning with greater and greater accuracy that the true core or our being, the essence of God/Self, has nothing whatsoever to do with sensory phenomena or with anything we previously identified our-selves with. It's worth looking at this progression in broad outline, to get a basic sense of what self-inquiry is about and how to go about it.

The *body level*, we might call it, involves understanding that "you are not your body." We all may know that losing a couple of limbs or getting one's face scarred does not destroy a person's intellect or personality. Most of us, however, are quite attached to our appear-ance and physical functioning, and would need to continually reflect on the impermanence of the body in order not to be.

> *Self-inquiry is the most direct METHOD—PROVIDED YOU ARE sold ON THE IDEA THAT the self is God.*

The *ego/personality level* involves all the conceptual mate-rial through which we distinguish ourselves as unique individuals: name, nationality, personality traits, aptitudes, memories, accomplishments and so on. All these things are fine and inevitable—but they need to be recalled and pondered repeatedly for us to really know that they do not define, or even color, who we really are.

The *psycho-philosophical level* involves what we do all have in common: the basic types of thinking, feeling and perceiving, and the resulting "deeper" concepts that are formed around what is means to be human: gender, sexuality, basic possessions, and other enti-tlements connected with the primary emotions (fear, love, etc.). Thoughts and feelings at this level usually go unexamined, and can only be understood and processed at deeper levels of the mind, through meditation.

The *ontological/spiritual level*, finally, involves seeing through the very core architecture of reality itself: realizing that even space, time, matter and causality do not condition or confine "who you really are" since, just like all those thoughts back at surface of your mind, *you* ultimately create them.

7   Singing And Chanting

This is one of the easier, almost universal practices which most anyone can derive at least some joy from doing. *Singing* here refers to singing hymns, which have verses that have meaning on the cognitive level. *Chanting* primarily refers to the singing

> *Since it involves vibration, the inner experience connected with any kind of music has a SPIRITUAL DIMENSION.*

either of spiritual texts according to a repeating melody, or more typically, to the repetitive singing of the same short phrases over and over again, often for an hour or more in some traditions. The object of both these practices, especially chanting, is to use tonal sound (vibratory energy) to effectively energize the inner power (Ch.10) throughout the body, but especially around the heart region. This often dislodges, at deeper and deeper levels, profound layers of repressed feelings and issues stored in the subconscious. Usually what results is a greater experience of overall bliss or contentment while the chanting is going on; however, a wide range of feelings can also surface in bouts of catharsis, depending on what the seeker is ready to process and is going through at the time.

> *Just as God/Self creates both light and darkness, music's energy can encourage some listeners down destructive paths if the GENRE IS CRUDE ENOUGH.*

A meaningful division might be made here between orthodox and mystical levels of practice. If you're singing verses, and their *meaning* inspires or moves you, that would be the orthodox level. The mystical comes into play when you're moved simply by the vibration or melody with no meaning involved at all. Most seekers experience both to some degree.

8 Breathing Techniques

By this is meant something other than ordinary breathing. These methods occur in at least some of the mystical branches of all traditions—Hinduism most of all, where it has its greatest development. They are based on the ancient insight of a definite link existing between the breath and the mind.

Even in moments of GREAT TURMOIL, *if you breathe slowly and deeply, you mind will* AUTOMATICALLY CALM DOWN.

Basic breathing methods are most commonly used for calming and centering, sometimes as an aide to various types of meditation when first starting a session, and sometimes as a meditation technique itself.

LAO TZU—*6th cent. BCE quasi-mythical founder of Taoism and traditional author/editor of the* Dao Te Ching. *He is alleged to have given up a government job in disgust and ridden off into solitude on an ox. Lao Tzu was later deified for popular worship; his poetry is amongst the most translated in world literature and has shaped the philosophical attitudes of millions of seekers. Traditional depiction.*

Less commonly, in the Hindu tradition breathing techniques known as *pranayama* take on elaborate form, with detailed time intervals and amounts of breath being inhaled and retained or exhaled and kept out, usually through separate nostrils. The more basic methods are said to balance spiritual forces in the body and can be done harmlessly. Advanced techniques, however, alter the distribution and intensity of those forces in the body and sometimes result in harm. What is tempting is that, for many seekers, these methods reliably produce states of extraordinary bliss and relaxation that the person may not be ready for. They do this just as unnaturally as any drug; the only difference is that a natural rhythm of the body is being temporarily altered, instead of its chemistry. The

> *ADVANCED BREATHING TECHNIQUES alter the distribution and intensity of subtle forces in the body, and sometimes RESULT IN HARM.*

verdict of many authorities seems to be that these methods often "burn out" or otherwise unbalance the mind if they are done for too long, and shouldn't be performed unless under expert supervision and with specific balancing or healing-related goals in mind. If such methods are done only for general spiritual progress, you may be rushing a process that would better unfold more naturally with ordinary practices.

9   Movement Techniques

Of course all spiritual traditions have developed *ritual movements* connected with their ceremonies and worship services; some of them extensive and complicated. *Artistic* and *athletic* traditions have also developed elaborate move-

> *Karate enthusiasts who break bricks and the like UTILIZE CHI ENERGY MORE THAN THEIR MUSCLES.*

ment systems relating to dance and rehearsal of various kinds (such as martial arts *katas*), which are thought of as having spiritual value. But there seem to be only two well-developed movement systems performed entirely for the purpose of spiritual practice: *hatha yoga* connected with Hinduism, and *Chi Gong* from Taoism (see also Ch.9,S.10). These days, Tai Chi falls into this category as well.[3]

Almost all seekers utilize movement systems at some point in their practice. Aside from producing better health and flexibility, theses techniques cultivate spiritual energy for better practice and healing purposes. Sometimes seekers experience this energy moving on its own, causing their limbs or bodies to move by themselves in various ways. More is said about this later (Ch.10,S.10).

Hatha yoga, chi gong and tai chi require training and commitment. *Simple movement techniques* for meditation comprise a different category. There are many of these—you can make up your own. Perhaps the best known is the *kinhin* practiced in Zen Buddhism, in which the practitioner walks very slowly and deliberately around the zendo (meditation hall) in a ritualized manner.

10 Study

To some extent or other, this is important for almost everyone and is ideally done in a spiritual atmosphere, and/or in a ritualized, focused way. Contemplating profound ideas through prose, poetry and story—whether difficult philosophical

> *It's not always helpful to study philosophy–atheistic material occasionally causes suicides.*

principles[4] or simple teachings and stories for moral instruction—is very helpful in reordering the mind's priorities and understandings. Insofar as it engages the mind, study is the primary technique for many who have trouble with more internal or meditative practices.

11 Ritual

Perhaps the most frequent mistake people make in their spiritual life is to overlook the importance of at least basic ritual. By ritual I mean a series of formalized movements, in general to begin and end a service or a period of practice. Without it, the distinction between a special spiritual activity and your everyday life vanishes. The thoughts, routines and mindsets of that life invade your sacred space and diminish its power. Flinging yourself around just any old way disrespects the body.

> *There are times for formality with God just as there are for the people in your life.*

At least a few movements, such as bowing, kneeling, folding hands and waving incense with a couple of yoga postures, or whatever—are essential for good practice.

12 Tithing And Charity

This practice exists not only to support good works and religious places, but also to diminish our attachment to money, which for most of us is quite profound and deserves a little explanation.

> *By giving money, we create a space for teachings to enter at a deeper level.*

Money not only enables our physical survival through food, and shelter, but is also part and parcel of the natural, positive attachments that we develop to our accomplishments, as good human beings and members of society. Providing for our families, being generous with friends and charity, and with institutions and concerns that we support, pay taxes or work for, as well as the things we own—all these things are the tentacles, we might say, of our karma, and they all involve money. Finally, metaphorically money represents toil and labor. A kind of subtle-emotional "bank" exists within, made up of all that sweat and cognitively linked to all those accomplishments. When we sacrifice some money, therefore, it "hurts" a little, especially when we do so anonymously and without knowing what is done with it, so that nobody thanks us and our attachments are not honored.[5]

> *Money is associated with sin because it wields* UNIQUE POWER OVER MORAL DISCRIMINATION—*you can buy and control almost anything with enough of it.*

Again, faith and good attitude come into play here. By giving money, we create a space inside ourselves for teachings to enter at a deeper level. Seekers at retreats and workshops often feel the benefit of this right away, provided that the spiritual agency involved is sound.

13 Pilgrimage

Whether orthodox or mystical, spiritual traditions occur in social contexts, and there is often a sense of romance connected with the language, culture and history of it all. To get over this romantic element you sometimes have to explore it.

That's the more superficial level of the value of pilgrimage. The deeper level has to do with the nature of reality itself and how we relate to it. In the final deepest sense, after all, the seeker is only looking for him- or herself. That's where the enlightenment is. That deepest self, of course, is identical with God and the

> *Cleaning and dishwashing* are ULTIMATELY JUST AS NECESSARY AS TEACHING AND HEALING *for enlightenment to manifest.*

universe, which means, again, that most of us have to explore that universe. For some people beautiful spots in nature are the most powerful places. For others, temples, tombs, birthplaces, and historical sites (of either factual or mythical events) do the trick. In either case, there seem to be deep karmic connections, in which we involuntarily *project* our deeper spirituality onto these places—and where it helps to go, if we want to take back the projection and make that spirituality completely our own.

BAWA MUHAIYADDEEN—*20th Cent. primarily Sufi teacher, Sri Lanka; later Philadelphia, US (d. 1986). (Hindu and Christian followers addressed him as "Swami," or "His Holiness".) He established a vegetarian diet for his community and welcomed people of all backgrounds. Twenty-five books have been transcribed from his discourses; the B.M. Fellowship has centers in the US, Canada, the UK and Australia.*

These projections, on the part of thousands or millions of seekers, over centuries in most cases, are responsible for the conviction that spiritual energy exists objectively, in and of itself, around holy places.

14 Service Work

The experience of performing some kind of work in the right spiritual atmosphere, for the purpose of supporting a good organization or following which directly alleviates suffering or promulgates teachings,

> NOT ALL DRUG USERS *are "looking in the wrong place."*

has always been an effective means of practice since it forces us to make spiritual teachings a part of our lives. Remarkably, it often results in the same tangible inner experiences that meditation and other more contemplative practices bring about. Insofar as it meets a demand and thus contributes a necessary aspect to society, ultimately any sort of work can be thought of as service (see also Ch.10,S.7).

Whether or not you are good at a particular kind of work, it can be said that the more kinds of work in different settings you are willing to at least try to do, the better off you are spiritually, since in that case you have no attachments to who you are and to what sort of work you should be asked to do. In fact, even the most basic things we do—eating, sleeping and so on—are work, in the sense that God wants us to fulfill our destinies as divine incarnate beings.

15 Substance Use

Historically this method has always gotten mixed reviews, since it's most commonly associated with addiction and other irresponsible behaviors amongst seekers who are "looking in the wrong place." Being an apparent substitute for God/Self, in one

> *If mind and body do not exist separately (Ch.9,S.2), then both drugs and bone splints* are ON PAR AS HEALING AGENTS.

sense using drugs is the greatest sacrilege: by getting high on our own, we implicitly deny that God cares or is even capable of enlightening us. On the other hand, natural hallucinogens and other substances do exist, and it's always been understood, or perhaps rationalized, that God put them there for a reason. Can you philosophically differentiate between a physical healing utilizing appropriate drugs, band-aides and splints, and a mental healing involving substances to alter our neurochemistry, if both these measures relieve discouragement or despair?

We need to sort out the different situations and consequences involved in substance use, for better context. It will be best to understand them theoretically, since the effects of a given agent vary from seeker to seeker depending on mood, ritual setting and so on. There are four "spectra" involved. Curious seekers should discern where they fall on each of them.

> *AYAHUASCA is the best known substance that seems to be actually transformational–enabling some users to* PROCESS PERSONAL ISSUES.

The first spectrum is reason for use. There are four: 1) recreational use for those less interested in spirituality, 2) developing faith for seeking agnostics (in which a person is exposed to higher reality for the first time, and develops conviction that there is something out there), 3) spiritual progress for committed seekers (see immediately below), and 4) relief of pain and suffering for the sick. One frequent failing many users have is a tendency to rationalize recreation as spiritual progress, since the person is "learning" about celestial realms, etc. If you use substances a lot, contemplating this may give you second thoughts about it.

> NEVER FORGET *that if you use mood-altering substances, it is at least partially because* YOU DON'T LIKE YOUR NORMAL SELF.

The next spectrum is whether a substance is merely *instructive*, or also, to some degree, *transformative*. Most of them merely show or expose the seeker to higher states of consciousness. As for the transformative category, some might be wary since you cannot tell ahead of time precisely what might be changed, or whether you could halt any such interior process once it was underway. A gray area probably exists here between these categories, depending upon the awareness of the seeker, or whether or not a qualified therapist, shaman or master who oversees the substance use is present.

The third spectrum is the degree to which there are greater or lesser harmful side effects on the body/mind. The most subtle of these stems from the fact that the seeker exerts no effort aside from taking the drug under the right conditions. As a result, to some degree he or she is involuntarily conditioned to think that spiritual evolution is always easy. There is

> *IF WE GO OUT OF OUR WAY to grow up more quickly, our destiny has no choice but to HAPPEN MORE QUICKLY.*

a subtle physical effect as well. Since the brain's existing neurochemistry is changed or supplemented, the experience is not entirely natural; the brain is "warped" or altered in order for the experience to take place, leading to problems later on with attitude and understanding when the drug must be given up, at least temporarily.

The fourth spectrum is the setting in which the substances are used. How much or how little has the seeker bothered to surround and structure himself with a good atmosphere (holy objects, etc.), teachers, company and appropriate ritual? This can make a tremendous difference in the seeker's experience of the substance employed.

16 Renunciation Or Asceticism

People give things up on the mystical path in order to find permanently, within themselves, levels of joy and contentment for which those things used to be important. This usually means less external stimulation.

Everyone does this, at least temporarily. When someone is upset about something, they usually seek less stimulation in order to deal with their feelings, which of course are connected with the person's understandings and past experiences. We can call that unconscious asceticism. The only difference with spiritual seekers is that the feelings and understandings they're dealing with are more long-term and general, stemming from disillusionment with reality itself. Life teaches us "what's really important" anyway, of course, but our lives do go faster as this effort becomes intentional on the spiritual path. More often than not, serious seekers take at least some measures to simplify their lives, in order to devote time and energy to practices and also to travel, change jobs and so forth for the sake of being around teachers, healers and the like. The challenge is in having faith in uncertainty (trusting God) that things will work out.

> *This practice involves a range of lifestyle modifications.*

17 Celibacy

As an ascetic practice, celibacy deserves special attention due to all the controversy that surrounds it. Priests and teachers practice it in some sects of some religions for a number of reasons. Politically, it prevents alliances from developing through

> *If you can't hold onto a relationship, TEMPORARY CELIBACY may be in order to better discern the "proper USE OF SEX."*[6]

marriages and liaisons that could compromise the group's mission. Occupationally, celibacy prevents the priest from devoting special attention and energy to a select few, when his or her job is to minister to everyone in the following equally.

NICHIREN—*13th Cent. Japanese Buddhist sect founder. To be sure he thought they were all misguided, Nichiren enrolled, ordained in, or otherwise studied every Buddhist sect in Japan before starting his own group based on the supremacy of the Lotus Sutra. He was harassed repeatedly, exiled three times (the third voluntarily) and almost assassinated. Even so, his sects now have an international following in the tens of millions. Drawing from painting.*

Spiritually, there are superficial and profound reasons to pursue celibacy. The superficial reasons are that your spiritual leader also practices it and says to do so, or worse, that you can't seem to find a mate. (Some people enter monastic orders for this reason, believe it or not.) The profound reason draws some seekers to this practice in spite of themselves. This is the slowly dawning understanding that the creative aspect of God/Self lives within us just as much as all its other aspects do. We are each "the being and source of all things,"[7] the wellspring of the cosmos and source of all joys. The whole universe is alive—wildly, ecstatically and unceasingly making love to itself in a shimmering overflow of pure creativity.

TRUE CELIBATES—people without any sexual experience who are nevertheless happy and fulfilled—ARE VERY RARE.

Most of us need at least some celibacy to begin to grasp this. At some level, some seekers realize that physical sex (and astral/celestial sex for some people who get into lucid

Probably 80% of all those who took vows NEVER SHOULD HAVE.

dreaming[8]) has conditioned them to a narrow perspective, and that for deeper understanding they have to back off from it, at least for a while.

Outside of monkhood, relatively few seekers intentionally practice celibacy. Most who do not pursue a sex life simply find that their spiritually related activities and interests are more fulfilling. They remain open to meeting a partner who might enhance even that experience, but often they never do. Most who do practice intentional celibacy, however, report certain benefits: a greater sense of subtle energy, clarity and focus, and of course a lot more spare time in which to do practices.[9] Most singles looking for a partner, or married people for that matter, devote a fair portion of their lives to everything involved in getting or maintaining the bonding necessary for a good physical relationship.

It is easy to understand the philosophical appeal of celibacy. It corresponds to the idea of transcendence, purity, spiritual warfare against our "animal nature," and focuses on that which makes us unique as a species (Ch.3,S.6); and of course widely admired teachers model it. But it's only necessary if the seeker's understanding of sexuality is confined to the biological or celestial realms. This is changing, however: people have more implicit philosophical understanding of different levels of creativity in the universe than ever before. The planet's spirituality is evolving and this is one practice that seems to be on its way out, at least in terms of formal vows. One unfortunate effect of liberal trends in modern society, however, has been to promote the idea that even very old people are unfulfilled if they do not have a sex life. It's fine for those who want it, but many others get distracted who would otherwise have benefitted from more contemplative interests.

> *If you can't help it, daydreaming is fine, as long as there's a DESIRE FOR HIGHER TRUTH UNDERNEATH.*

The final issue with this topic is the large percentage of prominent gurus and masters in the Eastern traditions who have broken their vows of celibacy (or otherwise misbehaved), creating scandals around themselves and their movements. There are two answers to why this happens. First, some teachers argue persuasively that significant "shadow" or unresolved issues can coexist with enlightenment.[10] The second answer stems from the simple mystery of being a human being. Enlightened people have individual interests and dispositions just like anyone else. One will like watching baseball and eating ice cream; another won't. Likewise, although equally detached for sex within, one will have a lifestyle and interests that involve a partner, whereas another will not. In these cases, the traditions of celibacy in which some of these teachers take vows in early in life prove to be too confining.

> *TANTRA MEANS "WEAVE"–as in different techniques and methods combined together, to SUIT THE INDIVIDUAL.*

Do either of these reasons excuse this behavior? No—but we are human beings. Celibacy is important for some seekers and can help them for a long time, but as a lifetime solution it's rarely a good idea.

18 No Practice

This is almost a superfluous heading, since some readers will have understood that, if the only practice you are able to do is recollection (S.4), then externally you're not doing any formal practice at all. To the observer, all you're doing is living a normal life with no apparent interest in spirituality.

Probably over 99% of seekers with serious spiritual interests do something by way of formal practice. However, if practices don't do the trick—if you consistently experience greater fulfillment while raising children, cooking meals, cleaning house, working part-time, running a book club, being engaged in civic affairs, etcetera—then that is a valid spirituality, as long as you at least try to recollect (Ch.8,S.4) as you're doing all that. (If you can't help it, daydreaming a lot is okay, as long as you keep trying not to, due to a connection and longing for the enlightenment beyond it all, awaiting the resolution of all your issues.)

UNUSUAL PRACTICES

The great majority of seekers never engage in these, nor are they necessary, but you do hear about them so they require brief explanation.

19 Tantrism

This is a very difficult term to define, because it has so many aspects. On the philosophical level, it seems to refer simply to the mystical orientation necessary for merging with reality through basic principles of cre-

> *Most of us interested in "spiritual" sex are better suited for SPRINGTIME FERTILITY CELEBRATIONS!*

ation as they are outlined in Hindu, Buddhist and Taoist cosmologies. On the level of individual practice, tantrism refers mostly to internal methods in which the practitioner identifies with the energetic union of male and female deities within the body, usually along the chakras. Mythical and iconographic elements of tradition are often involved, in rituals that can be especially elaborate at the group level of this

> *You can pray for a new car, but unless you do so with COMPLETE surrender, you're SECRETLY HOPING TO PLAY GOD YOURSELF.*

practice. The goal of the sexual techniques this term is associated with is to unite the male (*yang*) and female (*yin*) not so much physically as spiritually. There is coupling, but no orgasm or fluid exchange. The bliss connected with the experience is used to *unite the male and female principles already existing inside the body of each seeker*. This is possible because both men and women, on the spiritual level—just as they do on the hormonal and psychological levels, in fact—also possess the opposite gender polarity within themselves. Needless to say, seekers can't do this without exceptional levels of awareness, to say nothing of the training required and cultural barriers if one is not connected to the lineages and small groups involved.

20 Trance, Mediumship And Magic

For pretty much all mainstream mystically minded seekers, these things don't qualify as part of spirituality—they have more to do with the occult, which involves communicating with the deceased and investigating or developing talents with various paranormal phenomena. *Magic*, of course, tries to alter the natural course of events, and *mediumship* involves entering trances into in order to channel entities and spirits. *Shamans* use their gifts to actually intercede on spiritual planes to assist seekers in resolving their issues. A detailed understanding of these is outside the scope of this book.[11] The

> *If you SINCERELY ASK GOD for something, in essence you're trying to BE a magician— which is fine.*

main reason I mention them is that these practices often play a significant part in the world's indigenous religious practices, and in often more subtle ways are present in the major faiths as well.

INAYAT KHAN—19th / 20th Cent. Sufi Master, India, later Paris. Although coming out of an existing Sufi group, at his own Sheikh's encouragement Inayat left India and travelled extensively, founding the Sufi Order in the West and teaching what he called Universal Sufism. His son Pir Vilayat Khan went on to found the Omega Institute in New York.

21 Vision Quest/Rites Of Passage

For explanatory purposes these boil down to the same thing, as will be seen. These deserve mention due to their universality in indigenous cultures, and because of the popular interest which has developed for them in recent decades.

> *The purpose of the deprivation is to BREAK DOWN AND WEAKEN psychological defenses.*

Vision quests are best known as a Native American practice, and traditionally last for four days. The person fasts and purifies himself according to proper ritual, before the quest and during it as well. The younger the person is, the more important it is that elders oversee the entire process, although mostly from a distance. He or she is left completely alone in a natural place, with nothing whatsoever that could distract or occupy him, and no human artifice in sight. He cannot leave that spot, moves about very little and endeavors also to sleep as little as possible.

At first the seeker may brood, think, and have doubts about the whole thing. But gradually, as the hours, and then days, go by, all his worries, preoccupations, daydreams and involuntary fantasies play themselves out and begin to wind down. The person gets uneasy. Hunger weakens him. Boredom becomes more and more acute and bothersome. He leans against a tree, his head nodding involuntarily as he spends long stretches of time only half-awake. He is *not supposed to lie down* unless he absolutely cannot help it. (An elder stalks and looks on from a distance, to be sure things are basically okay.)

Native Americans elders DIDN'T WORRY ABOUT health insurance or being sued.

He finally does lie down, awakening a few hours later from an uncomfortable position. He pushes himself to his feet, looking at his watch. *Two whole days left!* He tries to pray and meditate as he has always done, but there is a void inside that he's never encountered before. His resolve is shaken, and he experiences real fear for the first time. But there is nowhere to go—only shame and regret if he backs out. He tries to pace, crawl, shift about on the ground as the hours drag on. Sapped further by hunger and insomnia, but also charged by his elders' encouragement and the gravity of what he is doing, he experiences a culminating moment of exhaustion, in which his mind finally collapses into what may feel for a moment like insanity—until God/Self breaks through from within, granting him some vision, epiphany or otherwise transformative experience which he otherwise might never have had.

If you want a vision quest with the rigor of "THE OLD WAYS," you'll probably have TROUBLE FINDING A TEACHER.

The example above portrays an exceptionally rigorous situation. You could say that vision quests are a way of "forcing the issue" of never having had spiritual experience. If undertaken with sincerity and commitment, however, God always cooperates to some extent. The mini-account above illustrates a hypothetical, determined seeker willing to push himself hard. There are therapists and spiritually oriented concerns who assist modern seekers in doing less severe vision quests, even for worldly purposes. Or you could do your own—a two-day quest, say, in order to resolve a relationship issue or business decision.

Rites of passage—which I will not describe in as much detail since they are otherwise outside the scope of this book—usually involve similar deprivations. As a young boy or girl, one day the elders come and take you away. Typically they blindfold you, isolate and starve you in a strange and scary place for a few days, telling you that you are no longer a child, but not yet an adult, producing fear and confusion.[13] Then physical trials commence in your weakened state. These might include circumcision, initiation marks, swimming a distance or running a gauntlet of spear points—whatever the culture's traditions decree. It's all meant to push you to your limits of pain and exhaustion, and then some. Finally, you get to rest and refuel. Then you sit in circle, and the elders welcome you into their brotherhood and formally acquaint you with the standards and duties of adulthood for your gender. Finally, you return to the village.

> *Because modern rites of passage are so easy, some teachers regard large segments of population as* NATIONS OF ADULT CHILDREN.[12]

What good vision quests and rites of passage have in common is an intentional stress overload of a particular type, designed to weaken the person's ego structure and requiring him or her at one point to "step into the unknown" and give (try, resist, endure) *more* than was thought to be possible. As a result, a great deal is learned and assimilated in an unusually deep and powerful way.

22 "Spiritual Powers"

These are not really spiritual practices, but are taken by some people as such.

Like growing up, progress in spiritual practice always involves an opening or freeing up of subtle internal capacities or powers. We had a certain amount of meaningful influence upon the people and things around us when we are 10 years old, more when are

If we are indeed God/Self, it stands to reason we could CUSTOMIZE OUR OWN DIVINE INTERVENTIONS.

20, and still more when we are 35. Spiritual practices merely speed this process up. As our wisdom and intuitive capacities refine, we acquire subtler and subtler understandings of things, and our meaningful influence on the world begins extending into what a 15-year-old (if he could get inside a 60-year-old's head for a moment) might describe, with awe, as the paranormal or supernatural.

The "powers" involved here are usually quite prosaic and associated with general maturity: a greater sense of presence, being more admired by or attractive to people, greater perception and understanding of situations, and so forth. Some people, however—perhaps because of minor imbalances, deficits, or excesses in their subconscious/spiritual character structure—develop unusual and probably compensatory abilities or tendencies,

To truly accept the human body, theology must EMBRACE THE FEMININE/EARTH ELEMENT, *which opens to door to "idolatry."*

which distract or preoccupy them for a while. One person might get into astral projection or lucid dreaming and have various experiences, some of them similar to those reported in NDE's.[14] Another might develop unusual sensitivity to people's feelings or auras, and occasionally experience spontaneous telepathy. Others might develop forms of ESP[15] and maybe go on to make their livings as psychics.

And still others, finally, get further sidetracked and develop some of the classic spiritual powers described in Hindu texts and elsewhere in mystical literature,[16] such as levitation, and use them to benefit themselves and others, if only economically. Again, that becomes what some of them consider their "spiritual practice," although to the extent that their egos are involved, real mystics would describe them as having left the spiritual path altogether.

23 "Forbidden" Techniques

In Indian spiritual literature, you may run into the term *Ban Marga* ("forbidden path") or *Vamachara* ("left-hand path." In many cultures, left-handedness is traditionally associated with suspicion or wrongdoing, since many of us around the world are still trained to do hygienic

It used to be thought in Europe that women's bodies were CONTAINERS ONLY, CONTRIBUTING NOTHING TO THE FETUS.

functions and other "dirty work" with our non-dominant hand.) Basically, these are techniques that *utilize* sense pleasures for spiritual practice, instead of avoiding or rationing them, which is the usual strategy. We've covered much of this already in our discussions of tantrism and substances above. There are other rituals among some small groups in the Eastern traditions (especially Hinduism) involving food and drink, as well as these other pleasures.

Early Hindu scholars named these practices "forbidden" because the obvious danger exists of practitioners becoming attached to the pleasures they are utilizing, and missing completely the divinity from

THERE IS NO TRUE MYSTICISM in the Church of Satan, since union implies HARMONY AND GOODNESS.

which those pleasures all stem. Some traditions even associate these methods with demonic influence. As a recognized category of spiritual practice, these techniques aren't found in the Western traditions (except among some Satanists, who pursue pleasures with a more or less selfish frame of mind as part of their doctrine), again because the philosophical orientations of these faiths, especially that of Christianity, basically isolates God from anything on earth or in nature (although, see Ch.7,S.2).

24 Crazy Wisdom

This is the term given to the attitude necessary, on the part of either masters or students, to intentionally violate social, moral and ethical conventions. Students do it to practice nonattachment; teachers to demonstrate it and, of course, to fulfill impure desires if they are unenlightened.

There is a millennia-old and honored tradition of social and political activism based on the "prophetic voice"—great spiritual leaders who speak truth to power and end up abused, in prison, or killed. This is the positive sense of crazy wisdom, perhaps most famously exemplified by Jesus Christ who, according to the Gospels, went berserk for a short time upsetting the gambling and shopkeepers' tables outside the temple in Jerusalem. (Nobody stopped him, presumably because

> *Unlike Jesus, if you started trashing blackjack tables somewhere, you'd quickly* FIND YOURSELF SUBDUED, AND IN JAIL IF YOU PERSISTED.

the Roman police were not there.) Various prophets in the history of the religions made themselves outcasts through similar experiences. On a larger scale, any of the more radical instances of modern social or political protest, such as that of the civil rights movement, or even the hippies in the 1960's and 70's, are in this same, basically positive spirit.

This term is more typically associated, however, with long traditions of occasional spiritual masters, especially in Buddhism, who misbehave in ways that are more or less universally condemned—typically excessive drinking and/or having sex with one's students. How this can square with spiritual leadership was partially addressed above (S.15) in connection with celibacy, but is otherwise beyond the scope of this book.

> *Some Jews and Buddhists find affinity because they each* FORMALLY QUESTION AUTHORITY—*Jews by* ARGUING, *and (Zen) Buddhists by* INITIALLY REJECTING.

Needless to say, the vast majority of Buddhists condemn this behavior like anyone else would. The main reason crazy wisdom occurs primarily in this tradition is because Siddhartha (the Buddha's original first name) explicitly told his students to reject previous traditions and authority unless it worked for them. Mystics tend to reject the cultural aspects of spirituality, and the Buddha certainly fit that mold. In saying that, however, he didn't mean to belittle or make fun of those traditions.

Responsible use of information tech-neology IS A HUGE CHALLENGE FOR SOME SEEKERS.

What this means is that some Buddhists are seeing something that isn't really there. As with any large group of people, some of them have issues with social conventions, which predisposes them to rationalize "crazy wisdom" conduct.

25 Dr. Frankenstein (Apps And Cybernetics)

One of the delusions of human nature involves the idea that we always benefit if we can do something better, faster and more conveniently. For example, when cars were invented, did we go out of our way to continue walking, exercising, and taking in the natural world? No. We built roads and cars everywhere indiscriminately, thereby contributing to crises later on in open space, global warming, and air pollution. The same thing is happening now with communications technology.

I add this as a practice because there have been more and more people in recent times (particularly science fiction writers) who think that enlightenment consists of directly supplementing our minds and bodies with genetic, medical, nutritional or technological advances of various kinds, until we are all immortal, indestructible, gorgeous, genius-level beings[17] who experience little if any pain. Nothing could be further from the truth of what is really involved.

JUST BECAUSE THE WORLD GOES FASTER doesn't mean we should necessarily keep up with it.

There's no question that information technology and social media have been an essential part of the planet's spiritual evolution. We are unified as never before. A global

> *On the individual level, overuse of communication technology* OFTEN SPELLS SPIRITUAL DISASTER— *and some of the greatest teachers have said so.*[18]

consciousness and moral conscience has arisen, and continues to develop as it never would have otherwise. But there's a dark underbelly to all this. My general impression—as a longtime fan of the *New York Times Sunday Review* section, which keeps us abreast of such things—is that some parts of the human population in developed countries, perhaps especially the United States, are more isolated, rude, sleepless, cynical, fat, illiterate, less social, less faithful, less outdoorsy, less family-oriented, less civically engaged, have fewer friends, and are more consumed with superficial aspects of pop culture than ever before.

The various subtle and indirect ways in which Facebook, Twitter, video games and the like contributes to these trends varies, but significant influences cannot be doubted. Computer in classrooms did not help test scores. Internet addiction is a real concern. Insomnia from trying to keep up with everything is more prevalent than ever, and attention spans are at an all-time low. For many, the tendency to isolate themselves in their own private selection of stimuli and influences has resulted in a kind of quasi-autistic abnegation of social responsibility. The result? Some people end up depressed, listless and apathetic without quite knowing why, from never having been challenged in ways they should have been.

Spirituality is about focused, emotional presence with others, face to face and in community.

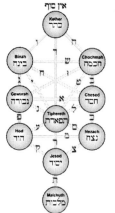

THE KABBALISTIC TREE OF LIFE—
Jewish mystical schema of levels of creation, of human consciousness, and of energies and spiritual centers in the body (often understood as a rough parallel to the Hindu chakra system). Courtesy Wikimedia Commons.

CHAPTER NINE

Health, Spiritual Anatomy and Yoga

These days health is a concern in Western spirituality. Up until the 1970s or so, when Eastern philosophical influence first became widely felt, this wasn't really the case. Ideas like "the spirit is willing, but the flesh is weak" reinforced the notion that the mind and body were separate. The resulting tendency was to not take any better care of one's self than a nonreligious person would have.

Mystics from both Western and Eastern traditions were often worse. This is because once God/Self is realized, the body is understood for what it really is: just another part of physical reality subject to decay and breakdown. So the tendency was not to treat it much better than you would anything else. St. Francis famously called his body "Brother Ass," and Nisargadatta (Ch.1), who lived in mid 20th century India, remarked, "it's not important that it [the body] lives long."[1]

These days however, modern sensibilities have impacted most enlightened people, and these attitudes are pretty much a thing of the past. It is recognized that achieving self-realization involves being able to perform spiritual practices diligently, usually for many years. Good health facilitates this undertaking.

1   The Value Of Traditional Systems

In the Ayurveda system of India and in the ancient texts of Chinese medicine, subtle-medical (for lack of a better term—see below)

> YOGA CAN BE THOUGHT OF AS *the mechanics of mystical spirituality.*

remedies and strategies are found for various conditions. Aside from their antiquity, what distinguishes these Far Eastern systems from any such systems devised in the ancient Near East and Europe is that their philosophical underpinnings are completely monistic—they understand the essence of the human being to be one with God and the cosmos.

Nowadays, many people in the Western world are familiar with the basics of these systems. In this chapter, we'll briefly look at the most significant spiritually-related understandings we need to have about health, the body and the mind; we'll look at the basics of subtle physiology, discuss alternative versus mainstream healing principles, and acquire a deeper understanding of yoga in all its now-varied forms as *the* mechanics of mystical spirituality and healing.

2   The Paradox Of Health, And Addiction

Health is paradoxical first because it is not possible to be *perfectly* healthy. At some point in life everyone suffers a bruise, gets a cold or has a pimple. Also, chronic health issues tend to be intimately tied to a person's cultural influences. This means that for many of us, nothing in particular has to happen in order for our health to decline in a way it would not otherwise have done.

Although they tend to be healthier than average, enlightened people are human beings and therefore have attitudes and preferences like anyone else, which do impact their health. Occasionally these can be excessive, even with no attachments.

> *Enlightened people are* EMBODIED BEINGS *and have attitudes and preferences* LIKE ANYONE ELSE.

We see instances of obesity, atrophied limbs, smoking, drunkenness, diseases going untreated, poor hygiene, over-suppression of desires and excessive fasting.

The phenomenon of addiction raises an interesting theoretical question concerning ethics, when it comes to enlightenment and the nonattachment required for it. Anyone is subject to possible *physiological* addiction. When certain drugs are used temporarily for long enough, the body adjusts to them and experiences discomfort when they are no longer available. Debate has always raged, however, over whether *psychological* addiction (resulting in less-than-honest "addictive behavior") always goes along with this. In theory, saints are completely detached from their bodies and ethically similar (see also Ch.12,S.2D), which implies that they can successfully resist being dishonest no matter how uncomfortable they are. But if the mind and body are deeply connected (see below) and/or essentially identical, then "the mind" would be subject to the same discomfort as "the body," perhaps leading to compromised thinking and addictive behaviors in their cases as well.

> IN THEORY AT LEAST, *saints are equally detached from their bodies and can SUCCESSFULLY RESIST DISHONESTY, no matter how uncomfortable they are.*

3   Deluded Buddhists?

Support for this is seen in Buddhism. In the context of the crazy wisdom behavior (C.8,S.22) associated with it, drunken masters occur now and then in a number of Buddhist sects down through the centuries; therefore this cannot be associated merely with cultish or otherwise "fringe" extremist groups within the faith. So, given the philosophical plausibility for it outlined above, it's safe to say that, under some conditions, even mystics occasionally behave in an ethically compromised manner.

In any case it does seem to be true that, when enlightenment is reached and all attachments go, there is a kind of relaxation back into normal life for many seekers. The diligence they maintained during their period of practice often abates. Again however, these days the great majority of teachers, and practically all serious seekers, understand that progress is facilitated by being as healthy as possible, and that "listening to the body" and sensing its needs is crucially important for most of us at some point or other.

> *Buddhism is somewhat unique IN ITS ACKNOWLEDGED TRADITION OF INEBRIATED, even alcoholic masters.*

JULIAN OF NORWICH—*14th Cent. Anchoress and noted theologian, England. With appropriate ritual to celebrate the occasion, she was voluntarily bricked up inside a small room for 40-odd years, until her death. She instructed followers from across the island, and received meals and the Eucharist through small windows. Some theologians consider her to be the first Christian "proto-universalist," teaching that God loves all people and wants everyone saved. Likeness of statue.*

4   Body And Mind Verses Bodymind

The philosophical assumptions at the basis of allopathic (mainstream) medicine for most of the 20th century were those of classical physics. The body was thought of as a mechanism that needed only adjustments of various kinds to keep it running. Hindu and Taoist thought, on the other hand, informed traditional healers in India, China and probably else-

> *The body's faculties for healing itself are* NEITHER COMPREHENSIVE NOR ALWAYS RELIABLE.

where of principles that Western medicine only began to appreciate in the latter part of the 20th century: the idea that the human organism has an inherent tendency to heal not only physically, but also spiritually, provided we take an interest and do practices. This means that, all other things being equal, you will be healthier physically if you chant or meditate on a regular basis than if you do not—and healthier still if you do movement techniques and follow a good diet.

To understand this connection between better health and spirituality more fully, we need to look briefly at an important feature of enlightenment. According to the descriptions, a major change that occurs once you get there is that there is no longer a perceived difference between the mind and the universe, including our bodies. In the self-realized state, we embody the cosmos in the most real sense imaginable, at

> *Imagine experiencing* NO FEAR OR ANXIETY AT ALL, *in even the most dire situation—although it may be* HUMANLY APPROPRIATE TO DISPLAY IT.

least at times when we're completely still during the day, and while sleeping at night. While moving about in daily activities, that experience apparently fades somewhat, but you basically remain part of an "ocean of consciousness,"[2] in union with all reality.

Unlike ordinary philosophers, mystics have always known THE MIND AND BODY TO BE INSEPARABLE.

In the enlightened state, although apparently there are times when you sit back and "think about things" in the normal sense, for the most part the "mind" no longer exists to feel things, because everything is *felt* directly already. And for the most part "memory" no longer exists in the way that it did before. You don't have any greater factual knowledge—the difference is that everything now is complete flow. All words and actions are "downloaded" instantaneously[3] from God/Self; there is no fear of anything, and utter, complete decisiveness about everything—even if the decision is to look undecided. The aliveness and abundant joy that you used to feel only in your heart or contemplative mind at especially powerful moments, is now experienced all the time, everywhere, and magnified far beyond what most of us consider possible.

So, whereas ordinary philosophers have argued over various theories of body/mind connection for centuries, mystics have always known them to be inseparable, even if the paradigms of thought didn't always exist to describe this union. (The description of enlightenment above has the mind vanishing into the body, but it could just as well be the other way around. The body vanishes into the mind—a headless state, if you will. Imagine your cranium expanding outward to infinity.)

In any case, the term *bodymind* is sometimes used in this chapter to be sure the reader keeps this merged experience in mind (no pun intended).

5   The Subtle Body

According to mystical and occult traditions, a replica of the body exists at higher planes of reality, usually called the *dream* or *subtle* body. Some amputees bothered by their phantom limbs

Traumatic feelings and memories are often "LOCKED UP" OR REPRESSED into various tissues of the body.

> *Many people in Zen REJECT THE CHAKRAS because they imply levels of progress. Their idea of enlightenment is that it is instantaneous and available to ANYONE WITH THE RIGHT UNDERSTANDING.*

call it their *ghost* body. Healers who do massage and other techniques sometimes see clients experience powerful emotions for no apparent reason, when certain parts of the body are worked with. So, these healers sometimes call it the *feeling* or *kinesthetic* body.

Needless to say, this is hardly an adequate description of the subtle body. In one sense, it exists "within" the physical body at higher levels of reality; in another sense it exists *outside* the physical body, since its existence penetrates higher dimensions which the physical body does not.

6   Chakras, Etcetera

The best-known components of spiritual anatomy are of course the *chakras*,[4] or spiritual centers in the body. Three different foundational cultures (Hindu, Semitic and Taoist) seem to have perceived and written up at least some of the chakras independently in ancient times, each with their own language, artistic representations and philosophical interpretations.[5] Other groups (Buddhists, Sufis, the Hermetics, Kabbalistic Christians plus others) inherited them from these first groups. Other features of spiritual anatomy, such as the *nadis* or channels in which spiritual energy moves, were also perceived and received similar interpretations.

Spirituality is a process involving different stages of purification, so the chakras are understood by the traditions to represent progressively more refined levels of vibrations and subtlety in the body. Details such as where they are located, their color, how many there are and so forth vary according to each of the three traditions mentioned. Without a doubt, these discrepancies were at least partially determined by the spiritualties, issues and artistic/literary preferences of the respective sages who first perceived and described

> *Experiencing our moods involves FEELING THE SUBTLE BODY. Enlightenment involves feeling "PASSIONATE" ABOUT EVERYTHING, ALL THE TIME.*

them. However, the larger and more important of these centers, as well as the *nadis* through which energy flows, always tend to be along or around the central nervous system—which makes sense, if we assume that the subtle body varies in function and composition from place to place in roughly the same way that the physical body does. Some healers see various other correspondences, such as some physical systems in the body being influenced by certain chakras.

Also, the subtle or dream body is not the only spiritual body, or "sheath," we have. Within it are more subtle bodies still. Again, the philosophies tend to differ as to the number of such bodies there are, usually from three to five. For our purposes it doesn't matter—it's probably more accurate, anyway, to speak of a single spiritual body composed of a sliding scale of subtlety within us, all the way to God/Self.

> *Characterizing Jesus with the chakra system* WOULD IMPLY TOO STRONGLY THAT HE IS A *normal human being.*

7   The Exception Of Christianity

Pictorial representations of the chakras, and of different regions of the body with different subtle channels or zones of energy are found in the mystical literature of basically all major traditions except for Christianity (except for the Kabbalistic Christians as mentioned). The reason for this is simple enough. A system of subtle anatomy implies that everybody possesses it, not just the sages who first perceived it. Characterizing Jesus with such a system implies that he is a normal guy (albeit an enlightened one) and not the unique messiah (another species—see Ch.4,S.2) that the orthodox faith claims him to be. A growing number of Christians do understand Christ this way, and have no trouble associating him with chakras and all the rest.

8   Healing The Universe In The Body

As implied above with the bodymind unity, the ancient texts in different traditions strongly imply, and sometimes say outright, that our spiritual body is a kind of analogue, or contracted form, of the universe itself.[6] If, as God, as the being and source of all things, each of us paradoxically *is* the universe, then subtle aspects of that reality are naturally represented in our spiritual body. And just as the external universe can be described systematically through science, so correspondingly to a less quantifiable extent can our spiritual body be so described. The ancients who wrote up the traditional healing systems mentioned earlier understood that for enlightenment to occur, the bodymind must undergo healing and spiritual processes to bring it into a subtle *correspondence* with the rest of the universe, so that the differences between the two can vanish. For modern healers, their systems have provided the basis for understanding how subtle dimensions of healing also correspond to physical and mental health problems as they manifest on the physical level.

> *"The kingdom of heaven is within you," and "heaven is a state of mind" are both true!*

SUN LUTANG—*19th/20th Cent. Renowned Taoist master of neijia ("internal" martial arts), originator of the Sun style of T'ai Chi Ch'uan, and Neo-Confucian and Taoist scholar. He published many works of neijia theory: the use of mind and spirit to regulate Chi energy in "soft" forms of martial arts practice.*

The work of these healers consists mainly in correcting *imbalances* in the way that our spiritual bodies meld with our physical bodies. Usually, our reactions to the normal affairs of life throw them out of alignment to some extent. Most of these imbalances are not major or outstanding, nor are they exceptional in the ways they manifest physically as various, usually chronic health

> *Someone who DAYDREAMS A LOT AND LOSES THINGS ALL THE TIME may be imbalanced in that he is not really "in his body," even though he has one.*

> *In the MONISTIC PARADIGM, disease is usually understood to have a DEEPER MEANING.*

problems. Other imbalances are exceptional or unusual. There is a longstanding concensus among mystically inclined seekers and healers that some severe mental disorders (which ordinary drugs can rarely do more than mask or suppress) represent different types of such unusual imbalances. Again, due to their understandings of how different kinds of blocks, misdistributions and so on of spiritual energy can aggravate or contribute to such conditions, alternative healers often can at least partially alleviate these disorders.

The only thing that distinguishes enlightened beings in this regard is that they have no imbalances that impact their perception and understanding of reality. Their spiritual perceptions of higher dimensions of reality are integrated perfectly with their physical perception. Other kinds of subtle imbalances, however, they are subject to. They suffer various health conditions and sometimes die of cancer just like the rest of us.

> *THE GOOD NEWS IS THAT, SLOWLY BUT SURELY, alternative and allopathic healing are merging.*

Alternative healers say that unusual frequencies of common maladies like colds, asthma flare-ups, and the like very often correspond to unhealthy behavior patterns that the person has trouble getting over; chronic or terminal conditions often correspond to deep-seated emotional issues. All this is linked to belief. Experienced healers are accustomed to seeing such conditions clear up soon as the ideas and issues in question have been sufficiently processed.

9 How Traditional Or Alternative Healing Works In General

This is relevant because it may get readers to consider an alternative healing strategy for a health issue, which could help their spirituality.

Two things render medicine an art as well as a science. First, people vary physiologically in all kinds of measurable ways—so much so that it's impractical for the healer to tally them all or input them into a computer. Secondly, everyone has a psycho-spiritual dimension of thoughts, feelings, and usually subconscious issues as well, which impact the way their body functions. This means that the best healing can never be entirely allopathic. The healer's subjective or intuitive judgment will almost always be important to some degree.

> *Two things render medicine an art as well as a science: peoples' unique physical make-ups, and the psycho-spiritual dimensions of their thoughts and feelings.*

Basically, for problems whose mechanisms work on the cellular level (like a flu), rather than chemically targeting it as allopathic medicine ideally tries to do, the alternative healer will administer something that either does not target the problem as precisely, and/or predisposes and strengthens the body to more effectively address the problem through its own defenses. What this means is that, at least for some conditions, alternative healing is better than allopathic medicine simply because the latter may have no specific cure for the problem; whereas alternative strategies may at least predispose the body

> *Unresolved emotional issues that aggravate or contribute to many medical conditions have an UNDERLYING INTELLECTUAL BASIS.*

to go about its healing more effectively. For problems that occur on the macro-structural level (like a backache), body-manipulation methods often do target the problem effectively.

There are four categories of strategies that alternative healers of various kinds may use. *Substances*: Herbs, foods, fluids, supplements, and the like help the body target or heal a problem, or cleanse it in some way. Frequently, patients have attachments to particular cultural traditions which factor into the exact strategy used. *Bodywork*: An extraordinary variety of ways exist devised by healers, ancient and modern, to manipulate, stimulate or otherwise enhance the body's own energetic capacities to heal. This is

> *It may not have been reasonably possible to choose differently at age 3, but you still chose.*

where many patients have their most eye-opening experiences if they have never visited a good alternative practitioner[6] before. *Ceremonies:* Many patients with certain spiritual interests or predispositions are powerfully affected by appropriate ceremonies with shamans and the like. This strategy can help a range of conditions, since the psycho-spiritual issues are addressed that were keeping the patient imbalanced or contracted in the areas of concern. *Counseling:* This element is much more prominent in alternative healing. As with allopathic medicine, alternative practitioners make sure that their patients understand their treatments and the things they can do to support them. But there's more to it than that, relating to the body-mind union discussed earlier: the importance of *belief* in determining the presence of a condition, or how severe it may be.[7]

AYYA KHEMA—*20th Cent. Jewish Buddhist Nun, Germany, then India and US. (d. 1997) Ayya escaped the Nazis and took monastic vows after marrying and raising a family. She founded many Buddhist centers, forest monasteries and the Sakyadhita, a worldwide Buddhist women's organization.*

The unresolved emotional issues that aggravate or contribute to a large range of usually chronic medical conditions have an underlying intellectual basis.[8] This type of belief system (such as, *my despair and anxiety must be ever-present because of how my father abused me*) constellates throughout the body as different loci of tension, straining normal tolerances in various tissues to the point where medical conditions develop which otherwise would not have. It may have been involuntary, but the people it these situations effectively

> *Some previous skeptics' newfound faith stems from* UNEXPECTED EXPERIENCES WITH ALTERNATIVE HEALING.

decide during their childhood that their bodies will suffer in such and such a way. Normal counseling just helps a patient manage the condition in question "from the surface," as it were. Good alternative healing however, with its spiritual element, *changes the person's deep-seated ideas (consciousness)* concerning the condition, "freeing" his body from it when tensions are relaxed thru the healing strategies. Otherwise, the relaxation only lasts for a short period of time, until the person's subconscious mindset tightens everything up again.

10 Yoga

There are many senses of this word—its overall meaning of "union," its designation of orthodox dispositional paths in Hinduism (karma yoga, bhakti yoga, etc.), its association with the "spiritual technology"[9] system of raja yoga, its use as a term for entire spiritual paths (for example, Kryia Yoga), and finally its best-known meaning as a system of postures (hatha yoga). In its broadest sense, yoga is the mostly systematic understanding of how spiritual processes and energies work in a human being to prepare the person for possible enlightenment.

In the end it doesn't really matter where yoga came from. Some Jews think that the ancient Hindus learned it from "the children of Abraham," and some Hindus think there's evidence that the ancient Hebrews' ancestors were of the same even older central Asian tribes who gave rise also to the peoples who migrated into India and profoundly shaped Hinduism. They probably all figured out basic yoga. Anyway, historical evidence associates it most strongly with ancient India; from there, it went on to impact branches of Buddhism, Taoism, Jainism, Sufi Islam, and Sikhism. Based on yoga to some extent, Buddhist and Taoist groups developed their own roughly parallel mystical systems of tantric practice and chi gong, respectively, along with adopting and modifying some of the original poses. There is little question that to some extent, the early Hebrews also had a movement system of their own.

> CONSERVATIVE THINKERS *in eastern* AND *western paradigms who appreciate yoga like to think that* THEIR TRADITION DISCOVERED IT.

ALLAH—*Arabic word for God (not a name). Superficial meaning: none. Profound meaning: "the word" in the deepest sense: vibratory surging-forth of creation. Sufis add the syllable hu for a mantra meaning "God himself." Courtesy Wikimedia Commons.*

CHAPTER TEN

Following Your Bliss: Understanding "Energy"

Very few terms are used in a more vague and general way than the word *energy*. In the most general sense, "energy" is relevant to everyone everywhere, because anybody, at any given time, can say something about the energy, or energy level, that he or she is experiencing, whether or not the special quality of *spiritual* energy is being discussed. The main reason this chapter covers as much ground as it does (religious atmospheres, initiations, spiritual masters, occupations, global suffering, bodily movements) is because the whole process of "following your bliss"[1]—that is, finding your own spiritual energy and treading your unique path to cultivate it—can involve a very wide range of activities, both inside and outside of spiritual settings.

Grace is God's UNMERITED FAVOR: the radical and transcendently mysterious expression of his power, prompting the recipient asks, "WHY ME?"

What is spiritual energy? When people say, "it didn't feel right to be there," or "the energy in the room was great," they are without a doubt referring to something at least partially akin to it. Human mood, language and expression are anything but rational, which is frustrating to some of us who either don't feel this energy, or are not impressed by what we have felt (or seen others apparently feel) in various situations. We *do* want to experience spiritual energy of the most authentic, meaningful and primordial kind, which is permanent and true, and which isn't just a refuge from anxieties or dependent upon favorable circumstances. And we start by understanding it as best we can.

The English terms used for this phenomenon vary, depending on the situation. In the secular world, words like *feeling, atmosphere,* and *ambiance* often refer to it, at least vaguely; in religious contexts, you hear *love, spirit,* or *holy spirit.* A more general term in the context of initiations, and of devotion and gratitude for its presence in our lives, is *grace.* We'll start out examining this phenomenon in more general psychological and religious contexts, and then go on to look at spiritual initiations, in which this energy is very often felt.

1   Spiritual Verses Psychological Energy

Perhaps the first question to address is whether or not an "energy" that you feel is of truly spiritual origin. The answer is that there is no way to tell, due to the existence of similar energetic feelings and enthusiasms we

> *It is YOUR ENERGY in the deepest sense, even if you only seem to feel it IN CERTAIN PLACES.*

have in connection with psychological and material needs. For example, when you are not in your place of worship, and you experience relief upon learning that certain special or unusual problems in your life have been resolved, that feeling can be quite similar to when you are in your place of worship, and you experience relief as a result of just giving over to God in prayer all of the usual issues and problems that you experience during your week. If you had been praying on those special problems outside your place of worship, you might have been inclined to attribute both of these relief reactions to God, even though an atheist friend of yours might describe obviously similar feelings from similar circumstances.

> *THERE IS RHYME AND REASON to the workings of spiritual energy.*

What makes this individual-psychology aspect even more obvious is that different people at the same spiritual event of similar ethnic background are affected differently by this energy—to say nothing of likewise similar people who attend different sects or religions altogether. One person will be hopping and dancing, another swaying gently, a third only nodding slightly, or whatever. The explanation "God works differently in different people" is obviously a gloss for something far more complex and profound, but which can be understood up to a point. Some consistent observations can be made, across all traditions.

2   Definitions—Two Aspects

There are different names for this energy—*Chi* for Buddhists and Taoists, *Ruach* for Jews, *Shakti* for Hindus, *Holy Spirit* for Christians. It is experienced in two different basic ways.

The first aspect of this energy manifests in a permanent, ongoing way. Some psychologists call it positive wellness; to differentiate it from mere lack of "disease"—whatever might cause you not to feel good in a general way. The more mature

> *Ultimately, this energy is merely a POSITIVE (or not so positive) QUALITY OF OVERALL EXPERIENCE, or state of being.*

we are spiritually, the more fulfilling and complete our experience of this energy is. We *all* experience it, however, as our general state of being (Ch.1,S.1).

The other aspect of this energy is episodic, most often occurring in places of worship, but also manifesting anywhere as different kinds of "peak experiences," and the like. The episodic sense is how most of us are accustomed to thinking of spiritual energy. In places or worship it is a temporarily blissful or otherwise euphoric sensation, often intense, which we assume to have healing, purifying or spiritualizing functions. This can be uncomfortable if it causes the person to experience catharsis (processing of feelings) as it sometimes does. More often it is not intense, however. Most worshippers experience spiritualty as a mild energy of unusual contentment; more rarely, it brings degrees of expansive joy and rapture with no tears at all.

The assumption and hope is that these episodes cause the permanent aspect of spiritual energy to increase and integrate appropriately into our lives. We will discuss this in detail, first in religious atmospheres.

REV. MARTIN LUTHER KING, JR.—20TH *Cent. Baptist Protestant theologian and civil rights leader, USA. He did much to bring about large-scale spiritual progress in Americans, through transmutation (kenosis) of prejudicial concepts. He was assassinated in 1968.*

3 Prosperity Energy!

An important observation to make is that, in both its aspects mentioned above, this energy obviously occurs at different levels of subtlety. The subtler the level, the less materially and psychologically based is the emotional or feeling content of what is being experienced or processed.

The *prosperity gospel* is an example of this less subtle variety. It is associated with Protestant Christianity but naturally occurs in all faiths, because many people's spiritual needs necessarily include some understanding of

> IT MAKES SENSE THAT GOD *relates to our practical concerns.*

how God relates to their practical concerns. God might be persuaded to do more for us than he otherwise would if we undertake extra prayers, works of charity, donations, and the like. This often involves *bargaining* with God/Self.[2]

The mentality here is hardly subtle, but it is a valid spiritual dynamic nonetheless. If God is both the source of all creation and of unconditional love, then part of that love should manifest as practical resources, provided that we do our part through faith, gratitude, good works, and spiritual practice. The fact that some religious clergy grow wealthy encouraging their audiences in this direction does not invalidate the worshipper's need to understand how,

> *For some, tithing is partially* a BUSINESS TRANSACTION, *even at the God-level.*

123

For some, what seems to be an entirely spiritual experience is POWERFULLY SUPPORTED BY PERVASIVE FANTASIES connected with money and material goods.

in whatever way, God does or does not provide for his or her material needs. In this connection, it is worth noting that the tithings that devotees pay at their places of worship do more than just assure worshippers that their clergy get paid and their temple's needs are met. Insofar as they and their institution serve God, there is the per-haps-only-subconscious expectation, which is not entirely irrational, that one is therefore less likely to be impacted by difficult or trying circumstances that life can bring.

In any case, *energy* in the sense of joy and enthusiasm is felt in connection with all this, which hardly needs explanation if you're convinced that God will reward you in exchange for your faith and support. Spirituality is present, but clearly psychological aspects are dominant in the often very animated worship style of prosper-ity gospel devotees. They typically get a lot out of verbal prayer, and are often powerfully moved by stories and accounts from those who have experienced the changes they are after. And there's fre-quent backsliding among these worshippers. In times of temptation and weakness, appropriate behavior is difficult because the positive thought content such a devotee often requires to maintain an ethical mindset is not there. The tendency is to experience strength and discipline mostly together with fellow worshippers, and to be more vulnerable out in the world.

4   Contemplative Energy

The worshippers above do experience aspects of spiritual energy that are too subtle for words to convey, but it is often a minor element. At deeper levels of spirituality, however, these more profound aspects become dominant. The devotee realizes that the most powerful prayer takes place beneath words, in total silence or through some mantra or rhythm

Like everything else, personal testimonies come and go, ONLY REPRESENTING A PARTICULAR PERSON'S CIRCUMSTANCES.

too deep to have a cognitive meaning. Stories are less important. Words and images don't matter as much because there's less interest in money and all the other things words represent, and the person's psychological issues, if any, are less pronounced. The constant, underlying aspect of this energy is felt more and more often, becoming more and more independent of the moods or feelings the person might be going through. As the seeker cultivates it, it becomes less dependent upon supportive circumstances, and the awareness grows that this energy is something, again, that everyone shares to some degree. The worship style, finally, is in general more still and quiet. Mystical devotees can be loud and animated and prosperity seekers can be reserved, but more often it's vice-versa.

> *A person's first major awakening CAN HAPPEN ANYWHERE.*

Below, in discussing the conditions under which spiritual awakenings take place, we must turn to the larger world outside of religion, in which people live and carry out their various activities.

5   Varieties Of Awakening: Finding Energy

An important question is how a seeker first comes in contact with this energy. Some people don't realize that they already have plenty of it.

One of the almost-universals that can be said about everyone for whom spirituality becomes a priority, is that they all have a *first major experience*, which can by thought of as an *initiation*, whether or not it takes place under formal circumstances. If not that, they at least have a moment when the *realized it was important*. A mystically oriented spiritual life usually involves an endless series of such experiences, but there is almost always one towards the beginning of

> *Obviously, some people with NO SPIRITUAL INTERESTS have cultivated a lot more energy than many who HAVE SUCH INTERESTS.*

one's journey that stands out.[3] Although it is more likely to take place around teachers and places of worship, this first experience, or awakening, can happen anywhere.

As to what increases the likelihood of such experiences, a distinction can be made between purely *internal* factors relating to belief, attitude, motivation, and suffering, and *external* factors which happen to a person, or which they voluntarily expose themselves to.

Internal factors are simple enough. The person decides whether and how interested they are in spirituality, and how much they are willing to do to accommodate that interest. (How much interest a person has depends on the depth to which certain phil-

> *Technology and environmental issues have rendered suffering* MORE INTERNAL AND WIDESPREAD.

osophical questions are contemplated, which may be an entirely subconscious process. Who am I? What is the purpose of life? What am I really meant to do? For more on this, see Chapters 3 and 4.)

6   Suffering, Disillusionment And Redirection

Everyone's spiritual awakenings, and continued breakthroughs, are to some extent catalyzed by internal pain. In orthodox religion, where people often get the message that God looks down on human frailty, this is exacerbated by self-reproach connected with one's own sense of sin. Of course, many people experience suffering from life on a personal level anyway (work, finances, relationships, health), without spiritual worries. Along with this, suffering in modern times is different than that of previous generations, in that it is influenced by a new and more powerful set of circumstances outside the individual's control.

These are mainly national and global issues. Worsening conditions in employment, education, medicine, the environment and other areas reflect shortsightedness in both electorates and their governments, and dysfunctions in the latter. Most of these huge, systemic problems have resulted from nothing other than the consequences of our own individual short-term desires and sensibilities writ large, so selfish by big-picture ecological standards. And we've long since reached the point

> *Irreversible and implacable change demands that we* REASSESS OUR PRIORITIES.

where that which is dearest to us is killing us. Where there are no opportunities anywhere, people are driven to create their own meaning and fulfillment through large families. As surely as the sun rises and sets, the populations especially of developing countries continue to expand and consume.

TUKARAM—17th Cent. low-caste farmer/laborer and later ascetic and teacher, Maharastra, India. "Tuka" exasperated his wife by giving away food and money, and endured business failure and death of family members during a famine. The best known miracle associated with him is the recovery of his poetry unharmed, after it was all thrown into a river by Brahmin priests.

In one way or another, the dawning realization that there are limits, and that we cannot stop polluting and overpopulating on our own without help from God, is indirectly contributing to more peoples' spiritual awakenings than ever before. Eckhart Tolle, a renowned secular teacher, recently said he believed we would destroy ourselves if a planetary awakening does not take place.[4]

As a result of all this, people begin understanding more profound things about life, often without realizing it. Interests and priorities shift. They might feel lost for a while (Ch.3,S.2),

> Obviously, POOR UNDERSTANDING WARPS this energy, resulting in religiously motivated NEGATIVE AND CRIMINAL ACTIVITIES.

at loose ends. Desires to start families (at least big ones) often diminish. They let go of previously held ideas about themselves and turn to activities of greater personal meaning, whether for personal fulfillment (college philosophy courses, big-wave surfing) or for relieving suffering or increasing happiness on the planet (literacy volunteer, animal shelter).

> *TRAUMATIC CUSTOMS (such as genital mutilation) motivate parents to MAKE SURE THEIR CHILDREN WON'T BE HAPPY EITHER.*[5]

The *greater energy* these seekers find in pursuing such activities is the same energy found by other seekers in churches and meditation groups. It is vital to understand this. If you grant that "spiritual energy" refers to the same phenomenon in all religions, and that it can also be experienced during moments of reverence at home or in nature, and that it can inspire people to do charitable works after the manner of various luminaries in the religions, then you must concede that any sincerely focused activity in which persons best express "themselves" in a process of pursuing greater happiness and fulfillment, involves the holy spirit. It's all the same thing. Mystics argue that everyone, sooner or later, gets enough perspective and understanding of life to realize that their spiritual evolution is the number one priority, because everything they do makes them more aware of it.

7   Energy In The World

The question may arise for some seekers, as to what kind of work or activity is appropriate. Here there is a tension between sometimes dated and oppressive *orthodox traditional duties* that you find discussed in scriptures, and more mystically related approaches. In the occupational sphere, for example, you find certain ideas in some of the Eastern faiths connected with not accumulating bad karma, to the effect that you shouldn't be either a farmer or a soldier, since both those jobs involve killing either people or animals; nor should you be a bartender, arms merchant, or anything else that might encourage or enable unethical behavior. In the domestic sphere, you would

> *If you're GOOD IN SALES but your product is FRIVOLOUS, where do you draw the line between LEGITIMATE COMPENSATION AND GREED?*

adhere to your duty as a wife, husband, child, or servant, and not test limits for the sake of fulfilling your particular desires and interests.

Mystical perspectives on work and activity are different. Three rules may be considered axiomatic. First, a person may move from one occupation to another, in any direction. There's no telling what the person may feel he or she needs to do, in order to grow. Secondly, by conventional standards, it may seem like the person is being lazy or not doing anything, which can be very misleading: inactivity may, in fact, be a slow gathering of strength.[6] Third, those around the seeker may be dismayed at what he or she is choosing to do, since it may not conform to expected norms. In order

> *SLOWLY BUT SURELY, most societies' levels of ethical sensitivity are CHANGING FOR THE BETTER.*

to reach a place of greater love, compassionate action and so on, the person first must transform him- or her*self*, which may involve doing things that seem quite selfish.

A deeper understanding of "work" undergirds all this. There are thousands of occupations in large societies, all of which must be performed to for those societies to function, and some of which involve seemingly controversial and destructive actions. Enough demand for something effectively sanctions it in the mind of God/Self. If your job is to repossess cars, manhandle drunk people, or offer your body to people paying for sex, these occupations can be performed with as much honesty and integrity as any other, insofar as there will always be demand for them—even if conditions make that integrity all but impossible. Other less dangerous jobs pose real ethical dilemmas, such as sales and other

> *PEOPLE WHO SURVIVE suicide attempts off the Golden Gate Bridge in San Francisco ALL HAVE SPIRITUAL AWAKENINGS on the way down.*[8]

areas that involve negotiating for personal advantage. Whatever you do, the major caveat is to watch out for psychological influences resulting from inappropriate greed, lust, or other negative tendencies.

8   External Assists To Energy

Following what was said above, I now briefly discuss *external* factors that can happen to seekers, and which they voluntarily expose themselves to in pursuing their paths.

These are many and varied. There are different groups of activities that create various *physiological* assists to spiritual experience.

These are athletics (endorphins), danger or emergencies (adrenaline), romance (hormones), and also substances (neurochemistry). Then there are *artistic* assists, be they God-created (the beauty of the natural world and universe) or human-created (music, drama, literature, visual art of whatever kind). And of course there are *spiritual* assists—teachers, places of worship and everything associated with them (Ch.12).

Common struggles with ATTITUDE AND MATURITY ISSUES constitute at least partial longing for god, since they ACQUAINT THE PERSON WITH REALITY.

All these things can aid and abet at least minor types of mystical experience. The final factor, of course, is fate (God) itself. What life has in store for a person, however, is intimately influenced by internal attitude and motivation. This becomes more and more apparent the deeper our self-inquiry goes—we begin to realize that through serious pursuit of spiritual practice, we are actually intervening and modifying our own destiny (Ch.11,S.6).

9 Ritual Requirements For Energy?

In the religions, there are commonly thought to be prerequisites for a good initiation experience, as well as for subsequent spiritual growth. Respected sources usually say that three things are essential: 1) a legitimate tradition with a track record behind it, 2) an authorized teacher within that tradition, and 3) a desire and willingness to sacrifice on the part of the devotee—that is to say, a *longing* for God.

Most people experience longing for God through EXISTENTIAL SUFFERING (which they can only blame on reality itself) and a sense of BEING LOST IN LIFE.

Obviously however (I say "obviously" due to recent issues in the Catholicism), people often do better spiritually after leaving an organization they were involved with. Nor are living teachers always important—someone with whom the seeker can interact and learn from in the most direct and immediate manner. Not only does full-scale initiation occasionally occur in dreams,[9] but the teachers—living or deceased—are often not anywhere near the person when the final enlightenment takes place. That said, the presence of living teachers tends to be very important, most of the time.

Longing is the only really important thing—and what's interesting is that the seeker may not even be aware that he has it. There are renowned teachers alive today who didn't really consider themselves spiritual seekers at all before their awakening—not because they didn't make progress through all the necessary personal and philosophical issues, but because they never thought of what they were going through as particularly "spiritual" (Ch.1,S.1; also Ch.6,S.5).[10]

CHOGYAM TRUNGPA—*20th cent. Lineage holder of Kagyu Tibetan Buddhism and originator of the Shambala Foundation, US. Although praised by his students (some of whom are now prominent teachers with their own followings) and by the 14th Dalai Lama—and giving reverence to the latter in return—Chogyam left monkhood, drank heavily and frequently had sex with some of his female students—and was forthright about doing so.*

10 Awakenings (Initiation Energy) In Spiritual Settings

It will serve our purpose to make a kind of theoretical distinction between an orthodox initiation and mystical initiation, distinguished by degree of psychological involvement. Again, this distinction blurs in reality but is helpful for understanding. It relies on the traditional distinction between the body and mind.

An orthodox initiation involves the mind. An example might be when young people are confirmed in Catholicism. With their early sacraments (Confirmation and First Communion),

For young people, religious experiences get lost in the "spiritual transformation" they are ALWAYS UNDERGOING as they grow up.

> GOD KNOWS WHAT WE CAN HANDLE. If our conceptual boundaries are stretched too far, we WILL GO INSANE.

Catholics complete their basic religious instruction and take their place in their parish community. The change and benefits involved in this are primarily psychological. The young person may feel exited or exhilarated up there in front of everybody, but it usually doesn't manifest as a permanently felt, inner transformation, primarily because as young people they are always transforming anyway, and have so many big ones yet to go through.

A great many religious rituals and ceremonies are like this. An orthodox initiation can only be effected by an institution.[11] It is, after all, "orthodox"—that is, performed according to guidelines set for a corporate body of believers. Both orthodox and mystical believers acknowledge that spiritual energy is effectively channeled through formal rituals sanctioned by the faith. At deeper levels, however, mystics experience this energy as inherently indeterminate and unpredictable. At those levels it tends to work around, outside of and through set structures and patterns, rather than conforming to them (the phrase "when you least expect it" is far more commonly heard in mystically-inclined groups). Such initiations undercut belief structures and affect the seeker's body as well. Energy is more often *felt*, usually as some degree of bliss or euphoria, but sometimes as uncomfortable feelings associated with catharsis.

11 Belief Structures And Energy: Inner Experience

Unless a seeker is enlightened, his or her beliefs always impact the quality and type of possible mystical experience. Until we get there, our attachments (beliefs) confine our experience within the boundaries of what we subconsciously consider to be possible. (For example, I don't believe consciously that the essence of David Low is a body that is white, in its 60s and weighs 130 pounds, but subconsciously I hang onto it in spite of myself.)

> The rigid belief that THEIR PATH IS UNIQUE in the eyes of God very likely BARS SOME PEOPLE from possible enlightenment.

The distinction made above between prosperity and contemplative energy is worth summarizing in the context of beliefs. The prosperity worshippers usually hold something closer to the exclusivist *traditional orthodox* view, which is that God looks down from above and decides how to implement his spirit in a given worshipper. In this understanding, God calls all the shots and all we can do is pray that he'll favor us. The more catholic[12] and mystical view favored by contemplative devotees is that God is always everywhere and that, all other things being equal, our psychological and constitutional differences, rather than "his will," is more often what determines how the energy will manifest within us.

> *For some, the FINAL BREAKTHROUGH is fraught with difficulty; for others, it's a gentle merging–depending upon what they DID OR DID NOT GO THROUGH UP TO THAT POINT.*

Naturally, the exclusivist experience is more confined, the primary limiting belief being that God exists mostly separately from the believer, making decisions beyond the latter's power to influence. There are certainly types of mystical experience associated with this, but they cannot possibly match those of a monistic believer, who at least consciously does not entertain this notion. Another common confining belief is the idea that one person, such as Jesus or Muhammad, is somehow unique or special in the eyes of God. This notion probably bars many orthodox believers from possible enlightenment, since it implies that there are two kinds of creation, instead of one.[13]

> *The simple, radical, astonishing truth and COSMIC JOKE IS: YOU ARE IT!*

Someone very close to enlightenment may no longer be attached to any beliefs, except the most basic one of all. This, of course, is the "I-consciousness" that the teachers always talk about—the independent, separate entity that dissolves upon enlightenment. It represents the ego with all its identifications.

> *How DIFFERENT are trances in spiritual settings versus trances in hypnosis-related settings? ONLY SO MUCH CAN BE RELIABLY INFERRED.*

Why is it so difficult to give up the "I"? Well, it is bounded, or circumscribed, by four things: *birth, death, time* and *space*. Remember, insofar as we each comprise an entire unique universe (Ch.5,S.2), everything in that universe and all we remember or anticipate doing in it—we identify with that "I"! Once we understand that *everything* out there is transient, the very parameters governing the existence of those things also collapse, and we *re*-cognize ourselves as God/Self. Until then, our understanding and experience are limited.

The remaining sections of this chapter deal with spiritual energy in the body and mind.

12   Belief Structures And Movement: Energy In The Body

The seemingly involuntary movements already mentioned (Ch.8,S.8) deserve more attention, as they sometimes frighten away people trained in traditional Western religion. To some extent, they happen to almost everybody on mystical paths, and for some seekers they are an integral part of their practice. As with other empirical spiritually related things discussed in these chapters, all we can do is describe them as objectively as possible, and make plausible inferences from what the teachers tell us.

> SPONTANEOUS MOVEMENTS *in spiritual settings are not always beneficial–occasionally,* SOMEONE HAS TO BE RESTRAINED.

The various physical movements performed by people doing spiritual practices can be said to fall on three different externally visible scales: how *fast* (quickly or slowly) they take place, how *smoothly* (flowing or jerky) they take place, and how *involuntarily* (total trance or total volition) they take place. The most significant of these is the last one—the *volition scale*, we might call it. At one extreme, people clapping and swaying while chanting or singing together may attest to the energy helping them move, but they basically still choose to sway and clap on those occasions, in the same way they would do so if they wanted to do it by themselves at home. At the other extreme, some worshippers

> MOST PEOPLE'S HABITS AND PRIORITIES *cause them to "leak" spiritual energy (knowledge and understanding)* ALL THE TIME.

in indigenous traditions enter a complete trance[14] (no memory of the event afterwards), in order to act out roles in some of their ceremonies. Presumably, both these examples are spiritually beneficial for their respective experiencers, although maybe in very different ways.

Perhaps the most interesting category of movement falls in between these extremes: movements in which the worshipper remains conscious, but allows the energy to direct his or her body as it will. Their eyes may be closed, but typically they can hear noises nearby. These movements can be stopped at will, whenever the person wants to end the practice period. There are three types of such movements: *yogic kryias* occur mostly in Hindu-related groups when some worshippers allow sitting yoga postures to take place; *standing movements* occur mostly in Taoist- and Buddhist-related groups in which Tai Chi or Chi Gong movements occur on their own, and *external utterances* (called "locutions" in Christian literature), in which individuals in different sects of the faiths speak words or create vocal sounds out loud.

BHAGAWAN NITYANANDA—*Early/Mid 20th Cent. ascetic, India. Widely influential through his disciples in the Western world. Because India is undergoing development, Nityananda represents a traditional way of life very likely in decline: that of the wandering avadhoot (naked) ascetic who, at least in the popular imagination, comes down out of the Himalaya Mountains and displays miraculous powers. Nityananda is thought to have been born enlightened.*

These movements are rare for neophytes. All three of them usually begin occurring only after the individual experiences either initiation or some breakthrough in his spiritual progress, meaning that a deeper level of purification is underway. Impurities of a very profound kind are said to released from our

KNOWLEDGE CAN BE BONDAGE, as well as power or freedom.

> *BECAUSE OF THIS ENERGY, spiritual settings bring out the best and SOMETIMES THE WORST in everybody.*

tissues in this process. For all these reasons, these movements occur primarily in mystical atmospheres.

We should note, finally, that voluntary movements are also helpful. The reason that practicing hatha yoga or Tai Chi is so relaxing and rejuvenating even for many people with no spiritual interests is that, although it may not be consciously done for that purpose, these poses still cultivate spiritual energy (which has become more "awakened" for those in whom the movements occur automatically).

13 Confined Energy, And The Consequences

An internal phenomenon needs to be described here which occurs primarily among orthodox followers, often impeding their spiritual development for years, decades, or even for the rest of their lives in some cases.

In mystics, spiritual energy always has a holistic effect upon the individual; that is to say, it works to interconnect and integrate all aspects of the person's psyche, both within and outside itself. Given that the goal is harmony and union, ethically this can only involve greater and greater levels of honesty and considerate behavior with one's self and with others (although "tough love" can be involved, insofar as people don't always know what's good for them).

Needless to say, this does not always occur among other people interested in spirituality, for two reasons. First, some individuals' deeply ingrained beliefs manifest internally as a kind of barrier, so that the integrating effect of the energy described above cannot embrace that part of the person's mind. Secondly, traumatic memories and issues, in order to be processed, must first sometimes be *activated* by this energy. This

> *In Catholicism, the idea of PAPAL INFALLIBILITY reflects an important philosophical principle, even if it is NOT TRUE IN FACT.*

often causes undesirable behaviors to persist, or even get worse for a while.

The most notable transformations happen when entire complexes surrounding such memories, and the confining ideas stemming from them, are transmuted by this energy (grace). This frees up realms of psychic energy that the person can begin using in more constructive ways.

14 Grace: The Master's Energy

Finally, usually in a more mystical context, there's a category referred to as *infused* grace. It brings the seeker to a palpably greater and often permanent level of happiness and fulfillment, and is often accompanied by an emotional reaction. It is called infused because it is permanently given, and is classically attributed by the experiencer to an external agency which he or she has gone out of his

In INDIA, your parents are traditionally thought of as your "FIRST GURU."

way to find: a special teacher, guru, deity, saint—or simply God himself manifesting as the external environment the person is in, which can be anywhere. Most of the time, a living teacher is involved.

This contrasts somewhat with some orthodox settings, where, for prosperity devotees (S.4), this energy is attributed simply to God, who wills it to manifest during worship services. Such seekers relate to this energy as being *around* them and temporarily energizing them, more so than inside (infused into) them. As noted earlier (C.4,S.3), the idea that God is within us is an idea which many orthodox clergy are uncomfortable talking about. This energy, therefore, is

Spend enough time in airport lobbies, and you will see young Indian émigrés TOUCHING THEIR PARENTS' FEET IN GREETING.

usually not thought of as permanent, but rather perhaps as "distributed" temporarily by God in the area where it is experienced.

Another important philosophical difference concerns the teacher/leader and the nature of the seeker's relationship with him or her. Orthodox settings are egalitarian in that enlightenment is not accepted and clergy are therefore regarded merely as having had formal training in the faith. More mystical settings are authoritarian in a subtle way: no matter how informal and human your relationship may be with the teacher—you may be one of his or her best friends or closest associates—the teacher is nonetheless believed to be enlightened. This means that in some sense, that person is invariably and always "correct" in what he or she says, although perhaps not in any literal or obvious way—especially because that very teacher may have some all-too-human failings. But the subtle authority is there, nevertheless, because it is *felt*—and also reflected in ritual actions, in which the teacher's best friends and closest associates will also bow, prostrate themselves, and so on, particularly in formal settings.

15 Devotional Versus Intellectual Dispositions

Regarding this infused grace, although these experiences can be construed as breakthroughs that seekers make within themselves, this is usually overshadowed by the powerful surprise element connected with the teacher's presence, resulting in strong feelings of reverence and gratitude. This gratitude, often for one master in particular, occurs in a large majority of serious, longer-term seekers, even with secularly oriented masters (Ch.12,S.2D). This level of transformative experience most often happens—some would say *only* happens—around living spiritual masters, which is why they are usually regarded as crucially important (Ch.12,S.2C).

> LONGSTANDING *mental structures are not surrendered willingly* OR EASILY.

No matter how objectively, internally and philosophically oriented a seeker is, the reaction of gratitude connected with the experience of infused grace is universal. Whether or not this gratitude is externally displayed depends on behavior conventions in the group and the individual's disposition. It is here that genuine spiritual followings are often confused with cults. The display of overly obsequious behaviors such as *gunga pranam*—stretching full-length flat on one's stomach—is usually not indicative of any brainwashing or psychological domination. Such behaviors are established conventions in societies where spiritual masters are prominent.

Even in more objectively oriented followings where such behaviors are not practiced, the same gratitude is nevertheless just as deeply felt. This is because the truth simply cannot be contained or understood by the mind. Longstanding mental structures are not surrendered willingly or easily. The pain of loss and pleasure of accommodating something much greater are experienced simultaneously when this happens.

BUDDHIST WHEEL OF DHARMA— *symbol of the faith. Superficial meaning: none. Profound meanings: eight-fold path that frees practitioners from cycles of samsara, reincarnation, the "six worlds," or the links of dependent origination. Courtesy Wikimedia Commons.*

CHAPTER ELEVEN

Communication
With God/Self

There are lots of spiritually related things that could be discussed in a chapter like this, because communicating with the divine relates to developing our inner potential: methods of creativity, meditation techniques, journaling, therapeutic methods with archetypes, and the like. For our purposes, we'll focus on two of the most important types of communication that we all experience the consequences of, whether we know it or not: dreams and manifestation.

Everyone manifests things for themselves, if only unconsciously, thereby forging their destinies. And there are consequences to not heeding one's dreams. Much has been written about these basic modes of communication between the individual and God/Self, but seekers often don't understand crucial things about them.

1 Dreams: Basic Backgroud And Context

How much credence we give to dreams and our motivation to act on them or not are largely determined by how we think they originate. It's certainly true that some dreams are not important, and it may also be true that they are partially determined by neurochemical reactions and other subtle physiological maintenance functions, which the brain carries out at night. However, spiritual and atheistic theories of dreams can both be right, applying as they do to different levels of reality at the same time. In any case, many dreams do seem to be important.

Conservative religious opinion in the West often associates dreams with demonic influences, since they frequently reflect private urges and desires and evidently come from deep within our minds, where our "animal instincts" dwell. Most seekers hold

Since different levels of reality are involved, dreams can be by-products of neurochemistry as well as productions of a higher spiritual intelligence at the same time.

more positive views, however, and are at least vaguely familiar with the prophetic, therapeutic or inspirational functions dreams sometimes have. What many are less familiar with is the mechanics of how dreams actually work in a spiritual sense. We may have heard

On the orthodox level, dreams are often associated with demonic influence in western religion.

that dreams and their symbols tell us important things about personal issues we're struggling with, but we are less likely to believe it if we don't understand how and why the dreams do it. This involves understanding in

greater depth what symbols are, and how they come into being in the context of our own creation.

2 Primordial Psychology I: Dreams And Reality

We need to first understand more about consciousness. Consciousness is simply experience—our reality in general, at any given time. Experience, however, has a *feeling-tone*[1] to it. One dimension of that feeling-tone is our mood, or how we're feeling in the normal sense, which is typically affected by the affairs of life.

A more subtle dimension of this feeling-tone consists of the deep-seated assumptions that, to some extent, most of us project onto everything around us. Someone who is always grumbling about getting ripped off or being taken advantage of will project a pervading fog, if you

With enough spiritual practice, all reality becomes a work of art—fascinating, and beautiful.

will, of resentment onto everything he sees, causing him to react to things in certain ways. (And often, therefore, attracting those unpleasant things to himself—but we'll get to that.) The point is, we are *always* experiencing a mood, connected with absolutely everything, even if that experience is undiscernibly neutral for most of us most of the time. This is true because we all have seep-seated assumptions of some kind or other. If you attend to your state of being, you will feel this mood in a subtle way, pervading your whole body.

Finally, there's a third, deepest level of feeling-tone, and here again you have to accept a paradox of enlightenment already mentioned (Ch.5,S.2): in co-creating the universe with our thoughts, we each exist at the center of our unique one. We may not be conscious of it in the unenlightened state, but we are each intimately connected with everything. That connection is itself the deepest feeling-tone experience we have.

So, we *feel* everything, whether or not we realize it. And here's where an important understanding about dreams comes in. Probably the main reason we may have read that dreams take place in a world of "feelings" or "emotions" is because they were studied and written about by the classic dream investigators (Freud and Jung) mostly in a context of wanting to help people therapeutically with their feelings and emotions. However, these writers did not subscribe to the monistic paradigm of thought assumed in this book. It would be more accurate to say that dreams take place in a world not of feelings, but of *half-formed reality* which we do indeed feel, whether we end up in therapy or not.

> *IT'S MORE ACCURATE to say that dreams take place in a world not of feelings, but of HALF-FORMED REALITY.*

The next step towards a good understanding of how dreams are connected to reality is to contemplate some other aspects of self-realization. Enlightened beings *feel*, of course, as fulfilled as it is possible to feel, since they are both God and Self. Paradoxically, they experience both the world of physical form as well as the effulgent reality beyond all form at the same time. This represents an indescribably more fulfilled and exhilarating *feeling-tone* of all reality, which they experience being the center and source of. (As human beings in the drama of creation, enlightened individuals might "act out"—although with complete sincerity—a sour mood if sick in a hospital or a good mood on a bright spring day, but inside they are touched by neither.)

SHAMS OF TABRIZ—*13th Cent. weaver and wandering Sufi ascetic. Would sometimes insult his audiences and offered close instruction to only one student—the great Persian poet Jalal'udin Rumi. He is said to have been murdered by some of Rumi's followers.*

Very roughly speaking, therefore, dream-consciousness can be thought of as a stage of reality halfway between the physical world and God. Things are fluid, half-formed, tentative. The laws of nature (time, space, causality) are likewise fluid, not yet set in stone. It can also be described as a "pre-literate" state of reality, since no languages exist yet either—although a specific environment and language "condenses" out of the dream world temporarily for the individual dreamer. As we all jointly co-create the universe out of our essence (God), it is as if the creative process, which determines our individual realities, was arrested at some point along the way.

Most of us are unaware OF THE DEEPER CONNECTION WE HAVE TO OUR *co-created universes.*

In the monistic view, CREATION IS ALWAYS HAPPENING—*meaning that we can influence it* MORE THAN WE THINK.

143

3   Primoridal Psychology II: Dreams And Creation

Now, one thing to remember here is that it's not really right to say that creation happened only one time, long ago. The monistic view is that creation is *ongoing*. All stages of the creative process—of reality—continue to exist. As human beings, therefore, we "inhabit" all of them simultaneously, our dream body existing in the middle, as it were. It has its own phase of activity over the 24-hour cycle, just like our physical bodies do.

At this point, recall the deeper levels of connectedness mentioned above, which we have to our physical realities in waking life. Although in one sense we have "full awareness" in waking life, most of us remain *unaware* of the deeper connection we have to our co-created universes, due to lack of spiritual development. In dreams, however, two things go on at the same time: we have

> *We don't have full awareness in dream worlds, because in them WE OURSELVES ARE ONLY HALF-FORMED.[3]*

less awareness overall, and therefore cannot usually control what happens to us in dreams; and we *are* aware of that deeper connection to half-formed reality. The reason we don't have full awareness in the half-formed reality of the dream world is because, in that state of existence, *we ourselves are only half-formed*. Every time we descend into the dream state after going to sleep, our entire organized sense of identity (ego and character structure) partially dissolves. In the deep sleep state, the teachers say[2] we almost dissolve completely and remerge with God/Self for a short time.

Spiritual practice is very important in this scenario. To understand why, we can look at four stages of creation.

STAGE 1: God.

STAGE 2: God begins to split itself off from itself.

STAGE 3: One half of God becomes a half-formed external reality; the other half of God becomes a half-formed internal reality.

STAGE 4: Completed creation: An individual experiencing his or her universe.[4]

Our normal everyday life, of course, is in Stage 4. But if we do spiritual practices in Stage 4, we increase our level of awareness in Stage 3. This means that we can control our still-forming external reality in Stage 3, since we have taken the trouble to develop ourselves faster than it is developing. And it will automatically modify its own direction of development in the way we want it to.

Your karma may be EASY, or it may be SISYPHEAN— everyone has DIFFERENT AMOUNTS of pain, trauma and conditioning to deal with.

That's the basic theory behind creative manifestation, and of how dreams relate to creation overall. How effectively you can change your reality, however, depends partially upon *what you have to go through.* That's your karma. It may be easy, or it may be Sisyphean— there can be no question that not everybody has the same amount of pain, trauma and conditioning to deal with.

4   Messages On The Path

Next we need to understand more precisely how seekers get important messages through dreams. Here's a way to visualize it.

Metaphysically, the word *karma* is used in two senses: 1) as the hidden complex of cause-and-effect which has *led* to a certain situation, and 2) as the "reason" for the complete set of circumstances an individual experiences at any given moment. In the latter sense a person's karma delineates all aspects of his or her reality. Within that, a certain range of possibilities could crystallize in that person's future, depending on what he or she chooses to think and do. The level of awareness the person has of his or her connectedness to those things, plus of the importance of positive attitude and of his or her essential nature as God/Self, all determine to what degree the person co-creates his or her future with God, as opposed to living life unawares and taking whatever it gives you.

To pick up on things God is trying to tell you, you NEED ONLY BE INTERESTED.

But, because we are human and have the potential for enlightenment, God/Self is always obliquely informing the person through symbols of options; of different ways that co-creation could go. To pick up on this information, *we need only be interested.* (This is an important sense in which God is always "knocking at the door" of our hearts. We have to take notice to let him in.) We

> *WE POSSESS A NATURAL FACULTY for discerning alternate future scenarios concerning important issues in our lives—IF WE WANT TO.*

get this information automatically because, again, part of our being inhabits higher levels of reality and is always perceiving things from that vantage point, making connections about practical issues in our lives through mechanisms that transcend time and space.

We can understand this further through a kind of mechanical analogy. Imagine that you at the center of an enormous sphere. That sphere is your "aura" which, at it's most subtle level, extends not just three or four feet away from you—which is how auras are usually pictured—but all the way to the edge of your universe. But think of it as a sphere.

Now ideally, nothing impinges or impacts upon that sphere; it exists in harmony with everything surrounding it. In reality, it never quite does—major or minor moods, tensions, and issues exist between you and others, whether living or deceased—and whether real or imagined. You think of them, they think (or you imagine them thinking) of you, things happen, you all make

> *Reality is classically described in Eastern literature as A DREAM IN THE MIND OF GOD.*

decisions affecting each other, and—to the extent that you care or are interested—you're notified of things potentially impacting you in dreams.

That happens because all of our "spheres" interact with each other in subtle and complex ways, usually without us realizing it. Here is where we understand the aggressive-minded person who brings difficulties upon himself. All we need to realize is that "thoughts are things" and "for every action, there's an equal and opposite reaction." Someone whose mental world is always *punching outward* from their sphere causes things to punch back.

5   The Universal Language Of Symbols

The core of understanding how dreams work involves knowing what symbols really are and how they fit into the scheme of the individual's creation. This is actually not difficult to fathom. Think of three totally different people: a 30-year-old American college educated insurance salesperson, an elderly Amazonian shaman who has never left the jungle, and the 12-year–old son of an Afghani terrorist who's already carrying an AK-47.

JUST AS OUR BRAIN STEMS all control the same instinctual functions, on a spiritual plane we all share THE SAME BASIC LANGUAGE.

RABBI BEN ELIEZER—*Jewish teacher and healer, and founder of Hasidic Judaism, 18th Cent. Ukraine. Better known as the Baal Shem Tov ("Master of the Good Name"), he worked as a schoolteacher, clay digger, wagon driver, butcher and tavernkeeper, all the while as a "hidden saint" before establishing himself as a renowned Tzadik. He spoke against asceticism, and wouldn't let some of his students read certain texts until they had achieved some normal benchmarks of life in Orthodox Judaism—such as marriage and children.*

On the physical plane these three are quite different, but on the mental plane they are fundamentally similar in great detail. Whether literate or not, they all have *similar generic mental images and understandings* of a great variety of things existing in their common universe. They all know what clothing is, what sex is, what food and water are, what the moon is, and so forth for everything else in the *basic world*, you might say. That basic world is represented in roughly similar images that they have in their heads. At that level we all constitute one giant organism which shares that generic basic world, in all its archetypal variety and detail, all

MEDITATION RESULTS in better health and greater self-knowledge; dreamwork can tell you WHAT TO DO IN YOUR LIFE.

of it connected by the God/Self that we all come out of.[5]

AN APP THAT CAN WORK in the abstract languages of our sixth sense[6] is PROBABLY A LONG WAY OFF.

Naturally, the specific images we each associate with any given thing in the basic world with will vary from person to person, because we've all been exposed to different instances or manifestations of that thing. For example, one person may associate "fatherhood" with warmth, stability and reassurance, while another mostly with drunkenness, fear and anger.

Now, if the father symbol were to express itself *literally* in a dream, you would just see your father as he normally appears. This is usually not the case, however. Symbols rarely express themselves literally for two reasons. The first is that we have to do our part to understand what our deeper self is trying to tell us. If we don't care at all, we don't deserve the knowledge. The second reason is that the symbol represents, at its most basic level, the *principle* or *template* of the thing it means to indicate, since there is more than one instance of that kind of thing in reality. So for example, if you were an African tribesperson, your father-template might express itself as an elephant, assuming your myths and legends portray elephants as having wisdom, knowledge, and capacity for nurturing and protection. If you were an affluent Christian from New York City, that template might express itself as a giant-sized Biblical prophet, maybe with a flowing beard and tender expression.

Finally, the range of possible interpretations that a dream is meant to suggest also affects the symbols in it. Taking one of the above examples further, if your father might develop a drinking problem in the near future because of losing his job, the biblical prophet might appear in the New Yorker's dream looking disoriented and wearing a giant, inverted beer-bottle cap on his head. In this case, the symbol is shaped by factors across time.

Dreams are usually one step ahead of conscious under-standing—UNLESS YOU DIALOGUE WITH THEM.

Some other principles agreed upon by most monistically oriented psychologists who work with dreams are that 1) everything in a dream represents part of the dreamer in some sense, 2) that there are usually a number of plausible interpretations of dreams, and 3) that only the dreamer—although perhaps after getting help with it—can really know a dream's true meaning for him or her. Symbols are often impacted beyond easy recognition by factors across time and space that are largely outside the dreamer's awareness. But there's always some extent to which constructive meaning can be accessed. With enough study, journaling, and persistent curiosity, dreams can be understood for the practical and spiritual guidance they are always offering.

So much for God/Self communicating with us. We go on now to see how best to communicate with He/She/It.

6   Becoming What We Think: Initial Perspectives On Manifestation

Some philosophical assumptions limit our ideas of what affirmations can do. The atheist who believes only in empirical science, and the religious conservative who believes that God made the world and exists mostly apart from it, have in common the assumption that we have no special

> *With appropriate feelings and imagery, we BEGIN TO ASSEMBLE IN HIGHER DIMENSIONS what will later manifest in our lives.*

inner potential of our own. The religious conservative believes that a certain type of potential does exist, but it cannot lead to the monistic concept of enlightenment and God must choose to awaken it. In any case, both believe that affirmations work only psychologically, helping us to remember something or do it better.

But most of us don't believe we live in a blind, mechanical universe only governed by inflexible laws; we do think we can change

> *Psychological methods often cannot eradicate "old tapes"—a SPIRITUAL AWAKENING MUST OCCUR.*

our destiny by utilizing a source that transcends the normal laws of psychology. From the foregoing discussion on dreams, some basic principles of manifestation will already be apparent. Most everyone in the helping professions agrees to some extent "we become what we think." But there is a deeper, psychodynamic observation also largely acknowledged: that although our mind may seem blank and serene, subconsciously we continually reaffirm our basic, age-old observations about reality to ourselves. This includes not only basic dimensions of existence like time, space and so on, but also bedrock assumptions about ourselves that tend to be negative, and are often shaped by early traumatic experience. Many of us who try assertiveness training or whatever, and use affirmations to try to change, end up still coping with the same issues because the "old tapes" in the subconscious were not erased and transformed into something more desirable.

7 Desires Or Surrender?

Again, for clarity's sake it will help to explain two different kinds of seekers, even though most of the time we're a mixture of both. This will help us to see whether and to what extent we should pursue manifestation techniques.

Some people have recon- ciled themselves, or surrendered completely, to their situation in life. They wouldn't have things any other way than the way they

> IF YOU HAVE the conviction that everything is unfolding exactly as it should, DON'T BOTHER WITH AFFIRMATIONS.

are now. Such a person has normal desires insofar as they live in a body and function in reality. But they also know themselves well, and therefore do not experience too strongly what we can call *inappropriate desires*. They're not enlightened, but there's a strong element of faith in their path through life. A lot of things have smoothed out for them. These seekers don't employ affirmations because they recognize that everything is unfolding exactly as it should at any given time—instead, they maintain a more subtle, ongoing vision of their future selves, with the awareness that they are continually stepping into the unknown to discover how and to what extent that vision will actualize.

The other kind of seeker doesn't know him- or herself that well, and hence does experience legitimate desires which are, to

> *Often SELF-WORTH ISSUES must be addressed therapeutically before affirmations HAVE ANY CHANCE OF WORKING.*

some degree, *adventuresome*, driving him or her to interact with the world in a normal process of self-discovery. These individuals are more preoccupied with future goals and can benefit from using affirmations with the right spiritual awareness and intent—and with great caution, because their own issues impact those affirmations, and may manifest all kinds of external difficulties they will have to work through.

SERAPHIM OF SAROV—*18th / 19th Cent. Eastern Orthodox Christian monastic. Some accounts of Seraphim mirror a theme sometimes associated with the lives of hermits: wild animals will visit them, presumably being drawn by the peace and harmony they feel. One account has Seraphim feeding and petting a full-grown brown bear outside his hermitage in the Russian taiga.*

Which of these, primarily, are you? If you're mostly the first type but are still curious about affirmations, there are good general ones you can do.[7]

8 Prerequisites: Deserving What You Want

We can't really expect affirmations to work for us unless, in the eyes of God, we *qualify* for the things we after. There needs to be the appropriate attitude and understanding of how we're going to use the objects that we want. This includes an openness

> *Continually contemplate AN IMPOSSIBLE QUESTION: IN THE GRAND SCHEME OF THINGS, does it really matter what I possess?*

151

to better understanding the true nature of the thing in question, including what it *should* do for you, versus what you might want it to do for you if you had it. Along with this there's the contemplation of whether, in the cosmic scheme of things, it really matters if you have the thing or not.

For example, affirmations can work for financial goals as they can for anything else. Needing the money to buy a car is a legitimate desire. It might be inappropriate, however, to have selfish priorities concerning its use, no matter how commonplace such ideas may be; and it may help to be willing to share it with certain others who need it, and so on. The car may only be meant to get you from point A to point B— meaning that what it looks like, how fast it can accelerate and whatnot is of secondary importance. On the other hand, you might be meant to enjoy the beauty and speed of a very special car. You can't tell.

> THE MECHANICS *by which affirmations work are similar to those which determine* THE NATURE AND MEANING OF OUR DREAMS.

And what is the thing meant to teach you? None of us knows for sure what we need to learn on the spiritual path, so we don't know what we'll be blessed with having. A person's superficial desires for a certain kind of mate, for example, may not at all match what the universe brings to him or her. (If it does, the lessons involved for you may be quite superficial, depending on your level of understanding and interest.)

The final prerequisite to going about effective manifestation for something you want is to already be doing all you can on your own to get that thing. If you've tried, there needs to be the satisfaction that you've given it your one hundred percent, and still to no avail.

9   Doing Effective Affirmations

One can find many descriptions of how to go about manifestation through affirmations, but practitioners often miss the spiritual/emotional core of what really makes them work. Here are some steps, and how to understand them.

1 Knowing what you want and don't want. What is important here is being as specific as possible, based on searching contemplation of what you really think you deserve. You can't expect the universe to respond meaningfully if you haven't put some effort into thinking about what you want.

> *Don't kid yourself about not needing any ritual, no matter how profound or abstract your understanding seems to be.*

2 An image, if only vaguely formed, of what you want in your mind. This will help you better conceptualize what you're after and relate to it emotionally.

3 *A feeling of enthusiasm and joy connected with the idea of already having that thing.* This is important. It is what links you spiritually to the divine/karmic forces that will bring the thing into manifestation.[8] Enthusiasm is indicative of the harmonization process that is taking place between you and the rest of the universe.

> *There are accidents— they just have messages.*

4 A short, positively worded phrase or sentence that can be repeated out loud or whispered. Don't just think it. Doing this creates a kind of "template" in the space around you—a field of magnetic demand, perhaps—into which the desired thing can start manifesting or assembling itself at higher levels of reality.

5 Appropriate basic ritual for performing your affirmations, and the place and time for it. (Don't kid yourself about not needing any ritual, no matter how profound or abstract your understanding may seem to be. To some extent our communication process with God/Self needs to be embodied or concretized, especially at first.)

6 Some "altar" representation of a divine agency with which you feel connected, as a focus of the ritual. This can either be an effigy of some sort (Christ, Buddha, etc.), or just an *atmosphere* you create through appropriate decoration within your sacred space.

7 Say a prayer asking that things go well, and for strength of mind if they don't. Affirmations are very powerful and can stir up a lot of unconscious internal resistance.

10 Questions And Answers

In a sense, we are always asking questions of God just by living our lives and thinking the way we do. Normally, God/Self "responds" to a seeker's life when it goes "off course" in some way. Sometimes this results from a wrong decision, but more often it comes from crossing a threshold. You might develop a need for something you're starting

> *God/Self* NEVER DEALS IN TRIVIALITIES *when it comes to inner messages.*

to miss too much, or an aversion to something you've started doing too much of. A certain food, environment, type of entertainment—when the time is right, you'll get a dream, hunch or feeling to adjust accordingly. Many people's lives don't turn out particularly badly if they choose not to heed such guidance, but the potential is there for everyone to move toward greater happiness and fulfillment, if they want to.

Again, many seekers experience pretty much everything unfolding exactly as it should, and don't feel a need to ask questions of God. If you lack a sense of this, however, and do want to ask, there is a general method you can use. All it requires is some faith in the idea that we all possess an innate wisdom that will "respond" if we can just bring ourselves to pay enough attention to it. Here's how to go about it.

> *There is a time and place* FOR FORMALITY WITH GOD, *as there is with anyone else.*

1 *Formulate your question.* The more specific and substantive it is (by which I mean: is it important to you?), the more likely you are to get a response. The same caveats apply here as for the affirmations explained above. Do you deserve an answer?

2 *Ask your question under at least minimally ritualized circumstances.* If you don't like the idea of an altar or have no focus for your own sense of God, then at least try to be in an intentionally quiet place or mood, when you ask your question. Writing your question in a diary just before going to bed is a good time to do this. Ask it again during a break in the middle of the day, as well as when you get up.

3 *"Chew on"* the question in a moment of silence. If you don't relate to prayer or meditation, then just maintain the silent awareness for a few moments that on some level, God/Self will assist you with this issue. Exercise faith. Don't think anything: just breathe, and be with that understanding for a moment

SWAMI PRABHUPADA—20th Cent. Indian Spiritual leader and founder of the International Society for Krishna Consciousness (ISKCON). He built a worldwide following and famously influenced the Beatle George Harrison's songwriting. When it was suggested to him that "God Consciousness" would be a better term for his organization's title, Swamiji replied that Krishna already embraced all other forms and concepts of God. Although associated with cult and "brainwashing" activity in the 1970's, the "Hare Krishnas" are a widely respected and well-established group today.

4 *"Submit and surrender"* your question. By this I mean mentally let the question go and be aware that you have released it. You can think of it either as sinking deeper inside you, or going out into the universe.[9]

> *To the enlightened, inner reality and external reality are the same thing.*

Discerning the answer to your question is the hard part. It requires continuous diligence, and realizing that it could come in any form or combinations of forms: conversations with people, unusual circumstances and events, thoughts and a-hah moments you have on your own, your and others' dreams, gut feelings, hunches, and so on. Pay attention in this way with enough persistence and faith, and you'll realize at some point that the universe has indeed "answered" your question.

CRUCIFIX—Christian symbol. Superficial meaning: Christ "dying on the cross for our sins." Profound meaning: what theologians call the Paschal Mystery: the energized internal principle of God/Self, to which the worshipper involuntarily "sacrifices" internal negative qualities, thereby experiencing transformation. Courtesy Wikimedia Commons.

CHAPTER TWELVE

Teachers And Groups

The best and most powerful spirituality has always manifested through human beings. A book or work of art might suffice for a while, but if you're serious about the spiritual path, you will be dealing with teachers, and with the groups of people who gather around them. The most fulfilling and powerful times in a seeker's journey are usually in the presence of such individuals.

Within this category, actual *living spiritual masters* are a concern. Generally, you don't find them in ordinary religion. Clergy in places of worship may be trained in knowledge and ritual, but gurus and masters—and many contemporary ones, especially in the Eastern traditions, are women—wield extraordinary influence through the transformative effect they have on their followers. The behavior of some of these followers, and sometimes of the group members in general, can be of real concern to some seekers. In any case, probably no topic in spirituality lends itself to more distortion than that of how various spiritual teachers, living or deceased, differ and compare to each other, especially since some masters themselves occasionally misbehave (S.2F).

I said earlier that for the sake of brevity, that few if any examples would be given of the things being discussed. That bears repeating here. Mentioning

> *Word of mouth is both the most RELIABLE AND MISLEADING of sources.*

individual teachers can do naught but mislead, since different seekers often have widely varying experiences of the same teacher, for complex reasons discussed below. The few living teachers I quote or mention in connection with possible enlightenment—as well as many of those pictured—may not be representative of it. Again, self-realization cannot be measured or quantified. What can be said is that, at some point, most all of the teachers pictured would claim to have had transformative experiences which completely changed their experience of reality (at least, the ones who come from cultures where spiritual enlightenment as I have defined it here (Ch.3,S.5&6) is a commonly accepted reality).

Before getting into criteria for assessing teachers, one capability they have in common with the religions needs clarification.

1 Who Chooses?

A well known experience in mystical circles is that of visiting an enlightened teacher, getting either formal, informal or *implicit* initiation (Ch.10,S.8-11) from him or her, and having the experience of *being chosen*, perhaps in spite of one's self. You may not even have met the teacher. Whether you wanted it to happen or not, you were powerfully and permanently affected by the person's presence. The energy or grace surrounding the teacher "included" you in its orbit, and you began experiencing a new level of spirituality in your life from that point forward. Other aspects of this are discussed elsewhere (Ch.10,S.14-15).

> YOU MAY NOT NEED A LOT OF FIREWORKS *to tell you what group or teaching to follow.*

If this never happened to you in spite of being around many such teachers, it may be because you've reached a level or type of maturity that does not require it. Again, some sagacious people never had any particular interest in God and spirituality (CH.10,S.9). In any case, it's not a difficult experience to relate to. While growing up, most of us can remember

> SOMETHING YOU *feel in your gut* MAY BE MORE MEANINGFUL THAT ANY *formal initiation ceremony.*

people we knew who had presence or were "powerful" in some way, maybe in the context of occupation, or family. Later on, we outgrew our admiration of that particular person when we saw that power in enough other people and began to experience it in ourselves. And we all get perspective on our parents when they no longer affect us like they used to. Many say, however, that the subtlety, power, and pervasive effect that truly great *spiritual* teachers have on them is above and beyond any such category of ordinary experience. This effect is almost invariably beneficial (S.2E).

What all this about teachers often has in common with orthodox religion is precisely this initiation experience. It often happens that seekers have an unexpected initiation experience when they visit a place of worship. Sometimes this happens in a setting that the person is completely unfamiliar with; from that point forward, it may become his or her primary spiritual influence for life.[1] In any case, the seeker is blessed or gifted with something they did not have before. For some seekers, this is the *first major experience* discussed earlier (C.10,S.5)—although in connection with a deceased and institutionalized master, instead of a living one.

> DON'T BE AFRAID TO CHECK OUT SOMETHING *completely unrelated to your cultural background.*

There is an overall difference between the two, however. Specifically meaningful experiences occur much more often with living teachers. The experience of grace from orthodox religion, verses that connected with living masters, does not seem to differ much in intensity, given how animated some religious people are in their worship style (Ch.10,S.3&12). But the living-master inner experiences seem to involve a greater frequency of meaningful specific content being revealed to the seeker, often motivating them to take specific action to address some issue in their lives.[2]

2   Types Of Teachers: Six Dimensions

It pays to think though the different meaningful indices, or dimensions, within which teachers can be categorized.

A   The first dimension might be *State of Enlightenment*:

1. Awakened teachers (enlightened)

2. Ordinary teachers (unenlightened and knowing it)

3. False teachers (unenlightened and not knowing it)

Certain circumstances govern whether or not a teacher ever actually says that they are enlightened. If he or she represents an established religious tradition involving previous gurus, they generally do their best not to say so, because it's important to maintain an attitude of humility towards the deceased masters. More secular teachers, however,

If you have trouble believing,
BE AN ANTHROPOLOGIST
and go anyway.

have no trouble saying so in their own humble way, because the whole atmosphere of reverence for tradition is absent and there's no danger of confusing or offending anyone through implied equality or superiority.

QIU CHUJI—13th Cent. Taoist master and popular lineage holder of the Northern School, China. After Pacifying Genghis Khan thru sermons (and likely saving millions of lives), the monarch appointed Qiu in charge of all religion in his empire. As a result, Taoism soon reached its zenith of political influence in China and beyond. Traditional likeness.

In any case, if enlightenment is claimed too frequently or confidently, or with true arrogance, you know to run in the opposite direction.

Although enlightenment in a teacher cannot be empirically verified, it is judged by certain traditional criteria. The most meaningful of these is *personal experience*. What happens to you in the presence of that teacher? Also meaningful are various *secondary sources*; namely, spoken or written testimonies from others. Finally, there is *institutional endorsement*, in which the organization associated with the previous teacher gives its stamp of approval to the new one, thereby lending legitimacy to the person through the weight of its reputation and history.

Personal experience, of course, can be both compelling and misleading. Different intensities of love, awe, fear, grief, anxiety, wonder, disgust, and so on are felt by seekers, depending upon their level of

> *Controversy frequently surrounds* ESTABLISHED TEACHERS DUE TO THE *purifying atmosphere* AROUND THEM.

purity and the issues they project onto the teacher. With this in mind, it may be a good idea to listen to the "average" experience of others before deciding whether or not to stick around. Even if the teacher is sound, however, and your best friends love him or her, he or she may not be the right one for you.

> *Underlying paranoias are the* FALSE TEACHER'S GOLD MINE.

Finally of course, the teacher also projects (presumably more subtle) issues onto the student, if the teacher him- or herself is unenlightened.

B The next dimension can be **Degree of Fame**:

1. Known to few

2. Known to some

3. Known to many

The consensus of highly respected teachers is that this is often misleading. A true teacher's style and mode of instruction may draw very few people to him, whereas a false or ordinary teacher's message and style may resonate with profound attachments and psychological needs held by millions. For this reason, the size or external legitimacy of a group may have nothing whatsoever to do with what you need.

C For our third dimension, we'll say **Age or Stage of Life**:

1. Childhood

2. Adolescence

3. Adult

4. Senior/Elder

According to both some widely respected world religions, as well as to some lesser known groups and lineages, this factor is also irrelevant. In some cases effective spiritual leadership can extend even down into early childhood.[3]

This is easy to understand if we can remember two things. First, if you're familiar with enough accounts of seekers achieving enlightenment, then you know it occurs over a wide range of ages, including some young people. It may be rarer, but in principle, therefore, there is no reason why enlightenment cannot occur at an extremely young age. Secondly, although we may stop growing up physiologically in our early 20's (which is when biologists tell us the human brain finally finishes developing), we never stop growing up in terms of worldly experience, enlightened or not. So, there is a sense in which someone who achieves self-realization at, say, age 25 continues to mature in conventional ways as he or she goes through life.

> *Given that enlightenment is enlightenment—the AGE OF THE TEACHER IS BASICALLY UNIMPORTANT.*

> *Religions make enlightenment into a MISLEADING BIG DEAL by calling it "SAINTHOOD," or "DIVINE UNION."*

The difficulty for some older followers of these young masters, of course, is that they may feel put off by taking direction from someone so young—yet they cannot deny the element of absolute and final authority that they *feel* from their teacher, which is beyond explanation.

D   The fourth dimension can be the important **Institutional Setting** (or lack thereof) associated with the teacher, which can be more persuasive than the teacher him- or herself:

1.   Orthodox established religion

2.   Mystical established religion

3.   Small groups or followings resembling major religions in different ways, but claiming little or no allegiance to them

4. New groups similar to the above

5. Secular groups

It will be readily appreciated how difficult it is to define such categories or distinguish between them, or even whether it is meaningful to do so. As implied earlier, some people need the legitimacy of a major institutionalized religion to accept a teacher, whereas others spurn religion altogether. Some observers think that the most encouraging phenomenon in spirituality over the last 30 years or so

> MANY TEACHINGS *of the major* *faiths come out of mythology* *or ancient history, and are* LESS RELEVANT FOR TODAY.

has been the emergence of widely renowned, basically secular teachers who achieved enlightenment in worldly contexts and who claim no allegiance to the religions at all, even though they may use teachings from all of them. The most typical setting that this kind of teacher works in is someone's living room, or a rented space somewhere.

In contrast to the religions, which utilize tradition, atmospherics and psychology (history, hierarchy, sermons, music, raiments, rituals, liturgy, statuary, pictures, architecture, group solidarity), these smaller groups mostly just talk. No pictures are hung or efforts made to create a special atmosphere. They focus, essentially, on what Hindus would call *jnana yoga*—the yoga, or path, of knowledge. Much of the time, however, nothing is explicitly taught. Instead, discussions take place

> ORDINARY PERCEPTION *of reality* *is just as important and* *accessible* AFTER ENLIGHTENMENT *as it was before.*

in which people come to terms with personal issues through greater understandings about life, in a natural process of self-inquiry.

E   The fifth one could be **Personality and Behavior** (which I think in practical terms are impossible to separate):

1. Austere and strict

2. Expansive and loving

3. Quiet and scholarly

4. Irreverent and mischievous

5. Etcetera, or any combination of the above

This is perhaps the most confusing dimension. Enlightened teachers have personalities like anyone else, causing seekers to prefer or not prefer them accordingly. The difference is that, at least in theory they are all equally *ethical*, although we have seen evidence elsewhere that this is not true (Ch.9,S.2&3).

And again, what does the seeker project onto the teacher? Brilliance, assertiveness, urbanity, masculinity, sexiness, an avuncular or fatherly manner, and other characteristics can deeply affect many people, in both positive and negative ways. The challenge is to disentangle your experience of the teacher's essential spiritual quality from your experience of his or her appealing personal characteristics.

> *There is a discouraging incidence of SEXUAL TRANSGRESSIONS among renowned teachers.[4]*

Another factor is *charisma*. This refers to the magnetic or compelling power possessed by an authority figure as a result either of enlightenment, *or* an outstanding gift for appealing to deeply held personal needs. Such gifts are not always good: Adolf Hitler was tremendously charismatic, as was 9/11 mastermind Osama Bin Laden. Both of them resonated with large numbers of people who had profound emotional issues shaped by the social and historical circumstances of their times and places. What is scary is that, if you look at the behavior of their immediate associates, you often find little to distinguish these politically related leaders from some spiritual masters in the religions.

RABBI SCHNEERSON—20th Cent. Hasidic Jewish Rebbe, scholar, and Congressional Medal of Honor recipient (d. 1994). After immigrating to the US in 1941, Schneerson achieved great political influence through charitable acts and was instrumental in establish the US Department of Education. An early proponent of solar energy, he is said to have worked 18 hours per day and "never had a day of vacation." In the latter part of his life he established "Sunday dollars," in which he would greet followers and give them a dollar bill to be passed onto some charity.

Anyway, you often have to stay around a group for a while to really discern for yourself if a teaching is good, or if a subtle imbalance or distortion of some kind is present that the teacher is unaware of.

> *Both political and religious cults involve "spirituality," in that the new worlds they promise are TOO IMPLAUSIBLE TO HAPPEN WITHOUT MAGIC.*

F   A sixth dimension, finally, would be **Appearance:**

1. Handsome/beautiful
2. Ugly
3. Well-groomed or not
4. Etcetera, or any combination of the above

Obviously, this is a meaningful criterion for some seekers, who in spite of themselves often project various sociocultural or sexual/romantic issues onto the teacher.

3   New Spiritual Movements

For seekers in indecisive situations involving teachers, there is obviously no sure criterion for picking one. Two things only are definitely true: a) teachers are important, and b) the spiritual path involves risk, and therefore faith. There are good apples, bad apples, and gray-area apples in between.

> *For some gullible seekers, things have to get worse before they get better— IF THEY EVER DO.*

It's also important to realize that in the first part of their history, new spiritual movements often seem cultish. This is because of the initial enthusiasm surrounding the teacher, especially in the Eastern religions where there are devotional traditions of understanding the teacher as an *Avatar*[5], or incarnation of God. Examples of unhealthy behavior (excessive genuflection, volunteering large sums of money) may abound, but that doesn't mean there's a problem with the teacher. Until the leaders put clear policies and procedures into place, it helps to approach such situations with awareness of just how powerful and transforming—and therefore, externally destabilizing—the presence of such teachers can be in the lives of some people.

Arguably HITLER was the greatest cult leader ever, followed by JOSEPH STALIN and other like him.

Unfortunately, some seekers do have personal issues that render them gullible to involvement with questionable teachers. Because the human heart/mind is one of the most, if not *the* most, complex thing in the universe, such issues can be so profound and convoluted that it may take years in a destructive relationship before some seekers realize how much they've been taken advantage of.

4   Cults And Gray Areas

Perhaps the biggest difficulty surrounding cults is the matter of defining them. While they are typically associated with religion, religion represents only one major type of spirituality (Ch.2,S.2). For example, some political movements also qualify. What all cults have in common is the mysteriously powerful influence of a central, leading figure. This person's influence impacts not just specific areas of the followers' intellectual interests, but their entire worldviews, including philosophical convictions that would normally be thought of as quite profound,

There is NO CUT-OFF POINT between the BEST cults and the WORST spiritual groups.

even in some seemingly mature individuals. As a result, standards of thinking and conduct can be significantly altered; infamously, people of different political or religious persuasions might be attacked and killed with no justification.

Because of the power of some cult leaders' influence, some theologians who subscribe to the Heaven-and-Hell system (Ch.7,S.4) consider the likes of exceptional leaders such as Adolf Hitler to be demonic on a cosmic scale ("the antichrist"). To be fair however, most cults do not have such sadistic or criminal inclinations.

SPIRITUAL SURRENDER involves risk—and RELINQUISHING TRUST in one's own judgment.

165

> FOR THE MOST PART, *there is a qualitative difference between SPIRITUAL MASTERS in the Eastern traditions, and TRAINED CLERGY in the west.*

Cults can be mild or severe, depending on how much and in what ways they exploit their followers. Some people, actually, are better off in mild cults since even as adults they have too little self-confidence or understanding in life to make their own way. And you cannot draw a line between the mildest cults and most severe "legitimate" religious sects (fundamentalist devotees, take note!). "Gray areas" are involved. Spiritual convictions and ethical issues which themselves are often murky—and which motivate such behaviors as going door to door with religious tracts—can easily cross a line into acts that many would consider pushy, if not offensive. Nobody will ever figure out exactly what psychological parameters and deficits cause some people to get involved in cults and some religious groups, because, again, the human heart/mind—the core manifestation of God/Self itself—is, according to the monistic paradigm, the most mysterious and complex thing in the universe.

5   Lineage

The final piece to a good understanding of spiritual teachers is to look at the concept of lineage as it has manifested in the religions, particularly in their mystical traditions. Generally, *lineage* might be defined as a stream of grace (teaching power and influence), flowing down through the generations of teachers in a par-

> EASTERN *lineages branch off and multiply, with LITTLE QUALITY CONTROL.*

ticular mystical tradition, or sub-tradition, within a major religion. Sometimes a lineage is said to be "unbroken"—that is, representing a continuing succession of primary disciples who, in real life, receive the mantle of spiritual power in a special ceremony from their teacher, before the latter passes away. Upon closer examination, however, this often proves not to be the case. Enlightened teachers in the religions often die without appointing a successor, or seem to appoint one only informally. In that case, the core followers have little choice but to form a leadership committee and do their best to represent the "lineage" which their teacher embodied. Historically, it also frequently happens that new enlightened teachers receive their initiation either from a succession of teachers to whom they were not completely dedicated, and/or internally, from and experiences in higher planes or existence with long-deceased teachers (Ch.10,S.9). Such new teachers may or may not go on to consider themselves part of the lineage that some of their teachers may have been associated with.

AMMA—20-21ˢᵗ Cent. Indian Guru and currently the most prominent female spiritual leader from the subcontinent. She was born (enlightened, it's thought) in a poor fishing village, had no teacher, and was continually chastised by her parents for giving away what few resources her family had. Known as "the hugging saint," her worldwide movement emphasizes service more so than solitary practices.

6   Ordinary People

It is often said by respected teachers that most enlightened people live ordinary lives and are not spiritual teachers. In terms of seeking, this is in line with the well known saying to the effect that we may learn more from the way a saint ties his shoes than we do from anything he or she may say. Such individuals exert a harmonizing influence that is usually only felt way below the conscious level, by those with whom they come in contact.

7   "Spiritual" Groups

There are a few caveats to look for in the bewildering variety of groups out there, be they brick-and-mortar and/or online. Aside from the teachers being okay, the main thing is to discern how much the group concerns itself with other things aside from spirituality.

Some groups are *political* as well as spiritual in their concerns, and may be associated with some cause. That does not mean that there's no enlightenment or that it might not the scene for you; it obviously does mean, however, that the intensity and purity of the spirituality is compromised, at least for those who benefit mostly from traditional practices like sitting meditation. Other groups are *psychological* as well as spiritual in nature. They do concern themselves with tool and methodologies for self-inquiry, but that inquiry has a practical goal: resolution of anger, grief, indecision, codependency, compatibility issues, and the like. Obviously, many seekers benefit from this, but it may leave you cold—even if you have some of those issues. That's because, in some cases a purely religious or mystical atmosphere maybe what is needed—your particular karmic configuration may require it (that is to say, draw you to it). Only then can you be cracked open, for the purification process to start moving.

> PSYCHOLOGICAL *methods may leave you cold, even if you have ALL KINDS OF ISSUES.*

Purely spiritual self-inquiry is intriguing, perplexing, and always to some degree powerful. "Progress" obviously takes place, but aside from bouts of catharsis over specific issues, you never have any idea how. Grace (Ch.10,S.14), which is an absolute and complete mystery, is the mechanism for that progress.

APPENDIX 1

About The Luminaries

I thought I would discuss the illustrations at the end of the book, rather than the beginning, in hopes that they'd be better understood when the reader finished. Again, they are meant to be kind of a parallel, more easy-going learning experience than you get from the text. I tried to include noted figures from all traditions who illustrate the variety of sometimes odd behaviors associated with the enlightened state. (Were they? Again, who can say for sure?) I also went out of my way to find women in traditions where modern female leaders of significant rank are still rare. In accordance with the supposition that enlightenment occurs in the ordinary world as well as the spiritual traditions, I include a few secular figures who were never primarily spiritual teachers, and who we would not normally think of as mystics. To avoid controversy (and for other reasons explained in Chapter 12), with only two exceptions I portray only deceased individuals. Finally, for some of the ancient and medieval figures, for whom no reliable or detailed portraits exist, the captions specify "traditional likeness," "drawing from statue" or some such.

And some of their behaviors are indeed intriguing. How must Sheik Nazim's intelligent followers have felt when Middle Eastern regimes were *not* all replaced by a ruling sultanate in 2011? What unknown psychiatric disorder must Anandamayi Ma have had, for her body to go cold when her husband made advances? (That one is anecdotal, but probably true—you hear of much stranger things in traditional India.) And after all Black Elk had seen and been through, how could he possibly have decided to become Catholic, of all things?

There's no rhyme or reason to it. The best you can do is to say that God is very playful and wants to underscore the fact that, again, our rational minds by themselves will never fathom the Truth.

APPENDIX 2

More On Meditation (Including How To Do It)

Most generally, meditation is simply complete focus on anything that you're doing, so that eventually, you experience the clarity and decisiveness connected with enlightenment mentioned earlier (Ch.9,S.4). In that sense all of life can be meditation. To develop that focus, we have to practice harmonizing the mind at every level until, with grace, it is strong enough to transcend itself in self-realization.

In most forms of meditation, the mind is not actually used at all, except to repeat or follow a simple thing of profound meaning. Some forms of meditation involve focusing on the meaning of a short word or phrase which does have a verbal meaning. Arguably however, this is prayer instead, since cognitive elements are involved. Meditation's goal is to quiet the mind to the point of absolute silence, consciously and subconsciously, so that it can resonate fully with its source (God/Self) and experience union. Since most people with a religious or spiritual connection meditate using mantras, I will confine my remarks mostly to that form of the practice.

Breathing

The most common "background" meditation technique, used by everyone to some extent insofar as they do it anyway, is simply to be conscious of, or to follow, one's breathing: the most basic of all body rhythms. This is our natural biophysical link to the rest of the universe, the most primordial "mantra" and very pulse of life, understood philosophically.

Again, in Eastern thought creation is ongoing; it never stopped happening. The astronomer's "big bang" sounds just as loudly now as it ever did, and our breathing (specifically, the space between the breaths) *is* that sound. On the biological level, it is the most fundamental movement of the life-principle that constitutes God/Self. The very meaning of the word for breath is many ancient languages is "spirit."

Hindu-influenced mystical groups often recommend repeating a breath-sound to your self mentally, as your breath goes in and out: SOOOOOO on the in-breath, HUUUUUMM on the outbreath. Something like that—or maybe HAAAAAM SOOOOOO. Whatever "sounds right" inside.

That method may help you follow your breathing. The trouble with breathing by itself as a meditation technique is that it is too "quiet" and unnoticeable, especially after it slows way down. The mind needs something more definite to latch onto.

Although all mystical traditions have naturally developed meditation techniques focusing around the breath, it is most commonly used in Buddhism, since that tradition went out of its way from the get-go to avoid giving a spoken name or verbal equivalent of any kind to the Ultimate Reality. And it's naturally suitable for many people with no interest in religion. Finally, individuals who merely want stress reduction often meditate on their breathing by default, without realizing it, since their stated intention is often to "just keep my mind blank."

Mantra

Together with our breathing, *mantras* are most commonly used. This Sanskrit term can be defined as "sacred word," or the "sound-body of God." Some people look at the Sanskrit root syllables and kind of expand the meaning of *mantra* into "that which liberates the mind," or "that which protects the one who repeats it."[1]

What's more important is understanding the principle behind mantra. It utilizes *vibration*. The very core of reality seems to be sound, or vibration, in the most profound sense. Sacred writings the world over seem to say or imply that the most basic level of creation came out of "the word." As the Gospel of St. John starts out, "First there was the word, and the word was God." From this *word* emerged *light,* and after that everything else came into being.

The best known closest verbal equivalent to this vibration at the core of reality is, of course, the Hindu OM, or AUM. In Arabic, Hebrew or some other ancient language, monosyllabic equivalents to this might be transliterated as HUU, YAA or whatever. They all verbally represent that core vibration.

By itself, however, OM (which the Buddhists also inherited) is again too indistinct for most practitioners to use in meditation. And so the ancient languages also have (naturally) *names* for God: *Allah, Yahweh, Abba,* and *Shiva* are some of them. These names, along with the vibratory syllables above, are typically joined to make the shortest mantras for meditation: *Allah Hu,* or *Om Shiva.* Note that, although some of these names are associated with scripture and story, in the more philosophical context of meditation, they do not have any cognitive meaning. God is indefinable.

Beyond that, it helps if mantras are rhythmic in a certain powerful way when you repeat them. Thus, the most common mantra in Hinduism is *Om Namah Shivaya,* which does kind of "spin around" or repeat itself in your heart/mind more easily in most peoples' experience than many other mantras of similar length (Try it!). It does have a meaning—"I bow to Shiva"—but that meaning is completely ignored in the profound experience of God that the subtle vibration of the mantra represents in meditation. It is six syllables long, which is about as long as you want a meditation mantra to be. Many people use mantras which are shorter. An English one, *Christ have mercy,* is four syllables.

In Hindu-related groups, this term can also refer to sacred writings of any length that are chanted, but it's usually thought of in connection with meditation. Western mystical groups use the term as well, since it was the first word known from anywhere that represents the principle of profound, vibratory essence. Finally, most mantras come out of certain *traditional languages* (Sanskrit, Hebrew, Greek, Arabic, Latin, Chinese), which are thought to be more powerful than modern tongues when it comes to spirituality.

Below are listed some other mantras from different traditions, all transliterated from their respective languages. (Exactly how to transliterate some of these terms is often a toss-up; since the phonemes, or sounds, is one language often do not have equivalents in others.) If a meaning is not given, they are simply names of God, and/or the vibratory essence. Ideally, you get a mantra directly from a spiritual master (which the author is not), but I have had luck in college classrooms with giving students lists, and having them choose one. So here they are:

Hinduism:	RAMA	
	HARE KRISHNA	
Christianity:	ABBA	
	KYRIE ELEISON	Greek for "Lord have mercy"
Judaism:	SHALOM	Hebrew for "Peace"
	HARA HA MAN	"O Compassionate One"
Islam:	ALLA HU	
	YA HA DIH	"O Guiding Spirit"

Visualization

Pictures of saints and deities, in all of their detailed and colorful regalia, are visual representations of the Ultimate Reality, which again, "vibrates" them (and everything else) into being. So, another major form of meditation involves a steady, sustained effort to *visualize* in your mind's eye, in great detail, a favorite saint or deity. Again, as the practitioner does this, his or her mind is drawn into the experience of inner bliss and union, forgetting anything cognitive (myths and stories) associated with the entity in question.

Induced And Movement Meditations

For people whose minds are too active for silent meditation, *induced* methods basically engage the mind and entrain it into a calmer state. The idea is to provide the mind with an external point of focus, since it is too scattered to maintain one on its own.

The most common (albeit too brief) example of this is a priest who guides his or her congregation in prayer verbally. CD players and I-pods with guided imagery, recordings of natural sounds or certain types of music can be very effective. The most basic way, perhaps, would to chant to yourself—that way, you don't rely on an external device, although you do have to be in a place where others won't be disturbed.

Movement techniques also provide an active mind with a point of focus, since you feel your body as you practice. You could do the Buddhist *kinhin* method or, in more normal life, simply walk for 20 minutes a day trying only to breathe and stare at a point directly ahead of you. Or you could get training in one of the movement traditions mentioned (Ch.8,S.9). Again, the aim here is to cultivate, stimulate or awaken spiritual energy in the body. Practice this, and you'll eventually be able to meditate sitting down.

Performing Your Meditation

For the spiritually inclined, the ideal ingredients are simple enough: an "altar" space (Ch.11,S.9), basic ritual (Ch.8,S.10,), and a dark and quiet room—some people like either basements or top floors, because of what they suggest metaphorically. Other ideal ingredients include a natural state of one's body (no drug use), an empty stomach (digestion requires a surprising amount of energy), being well rested (good meditation requires alertness), a meditation technique, and the quietest time of day—the early morning. In Indian thought, the *sandyas*—the precise time intervals when the sun is rising and setting, are thought to be good times, since everything is said to be calm and in balance when this happens.

As far as what to actually do inside, perform your technique, until you no longer need one! If your mind wanders, simply resume the technique as soon as you remember. That's all I feel competent to say about meditation. The trials, errors, and vagaries of the process itself will teach you what you need to "know" about it.

APPENDIX 3

Important Perspectives
On The Religions

In this appendix I explain some things about the different religions that some seekers may find valuable. Given that we're stuck with educations that often tell us how different the faiths are, we need less well known historical and philosophical observations to the effect that the religions all have the same, underlying dimensions of understanding and practice. We also need honesty, in order to call a spade a spade and not worry about political correctness. Without that honesty we will disagree, staying stuck in language and culture and never perceiving the deeper truth underneath.

Organized religion involves history, politics and other fields that can never be completely divorced from spirituality, because spirituality ultimately embraces everything. Seekers are often discouraged from pursuing their spiritual interests because of all the religion-related dramas in the world. Of course, many of them are involved in those religions as well—psychologically, if not in practice—clinging to various notions involved in those dramas in spite of themselves. Therefore, maybe these insights can help their understanding in some cases.

Finally, when discussing sociopolitical issues I limit myself to the Western faiths, since historically they were exclusivist and often proselytized by force. By and large, the Eastern faiths never did this, and so do not have nearly as much historical and political "baggage" that needs to be understood.

The Founders' Similarities

To varying degrees, what the founders of most of the faiths really taught their immediate followers is not, in fact, what their religions' most widely read scriptures actually say. These were written later, again in a way meant to be understood by anyone. The principles and practices which these first sages taught were often too subtle and profound for most people's level of interest. As mystics, they possessed the highest level of ethical and philosophical sophistication, which paradoxically does not rely on literacy—what their disciples learned was felt directly, imbibed more thoroughly, and led to enlightenment more quickly than for most of us, even today. These teachings didn't rely on scriptures, rituals, priesthoods, monasticism, prayers, hymns, giving to charity or celebrating holy days. All that came later, in the ensuing decades and centuries after the founders' deaths, in what scholars sometimes call the "religionmaking" process. Various luminaries (commentators, artists, storytellers, musicians) encountered the original teachings and began building stuff around them, in order that more average and less interested people could relate to it in a fulfilling way.

What this implies is that the founders themselves were, in all great likelihood, remarkably similar in their tone and method of teaching. They were, so to speak, "noble savages,"[1] elemental human beings with all pretenses stripped away, but possessed with the greatest and most nuanced and perception of reality, being in direct and innocent contact with it. They cried sincerely, laughed uproariously, were dead serious when necessary and could accommodate any sincere student's needs, with no attachment to the ideas and concepts they used. They would teach the same thing, either systematically or through myth, according to what they sensed their individual students needed.

In terms of what they have to deal with, the major sociological differences between the founders of the religions in ancient times, and modern mystics who teach today, are probably that the latter have a lot more competition and have to deal with a much stronger climate of faithlessness and cynicism. The modern media is largely responsible for both of these differences.

East-West Complimentarity

Certain complementarities exist between the Eastern and Western faiths, which would eliminate much confusion if they were better understood. Eastern scriptures and teachings focus more on *natural processes*, and the West more on *civilization,* or the affairs of humankind.

As perceived by the ancients, natural processes involved understanding the most profound "laws of nature," in the sense of how the universe works. Hence they have a more mechanical view of the universe than the Western religions do, projecting beyond our lifetime into the past and future with karma and reincarnation in the same way (although not with the same precision) that astronomers calculate the long orbits of comets and asteroids. The background assumption is that everything and everybody returns to God eventually, so that everyone who dies unenlightened must "reincarnate" in some sense to get there. The Eastern traditions, therefore, involve *natural* things typically outside the bounds of civilized sensibilities: animal deities, unabashed pictures, sculptures etc. of sexual intercourse, astrological systems and so on.

In the western traditions, events in an individual's lifetime before and after his or her physical existence on earth are thought more to be "God's territory"—we cannot understand as concretely what happens at those times, nor is it really appropriate to try to do so. In the bible, nature is appreciated in places, but tends to be associated with what religious people need to watch out for: aggression and promiscuity (mating behavior in animals), uncleanliness (excretory/birth/ menstrual/sexual fluids, etc.), as well as idolatry—the tendency to deify impressive natural phenomena such as volcanoes, elephants and the like.

This biblical view may seem to be an overly restricted orientation toward God—and many people of course think it is—but it does have its advantages. Mainly, we get a detailed portrayal of how God/Self manifests, on the assumption that he/she/it concerns itself primarily with humans and human civilization. The basic dimensions of how God would manifest in moral code and legal convention are detailed in the longstanding, more conservative interpretations of Judeo-Christian and Islamic thought. From this has flowed the comprehensive range of laws, customs and mores that ideally structure civilization.

Overall, we can say that the Western traditions emphasize *propriety* (as in, good behavior), and in that way are fundamentally more conservative than the Eastern religions, which more readily incorporate sexuality, "graven images," and reverence for the environment, since they deify so many things in it (all of this encouraging more questionable behavior). And so, Godliness in Abrahamic tradition means transcending nature, wanting to set ourselves apart from it.

Morally and ethically, transcendence implies superiority, and along with it the options of controlling, fixing and harnessing the natural world as we see fit, rather than utilizing it in ways more consistent with its own harmony, as we are only now starting to do. This is the profound origin of the more developed technologies of Western cultures, above and beyond the more primitive and basic technologies originally found in Eastern and indigenous cultures. As the Tower of Babel myth in the Old Testament points out, in pursuing technology we are unconsciously trying to reach God. By contrast, Eastern and indigenous orientations essentially view themselves as only one part of a grand spiritual ecosystem, pulsing with the rhythms of nature.

Scriptural differences support the distinction made above. If you read a Western document (Hebrew Bible, New Testament, Qur'an), you're more likely to encounter things like a single God teaching laws and ethical codes to groups of people, clashes between people or groups of people in some God-motivated political context, or teachings and parables which are largely earthbound—occurring in everyday situations with little magic or otherwise fantastical or mythical content. Eastern scriptures are different.

You'll see stories of different deities, sometimes connected with the elements or heavenly bodies; or descriptions of principles of nature or of subtle forces in the physical body; of highly mythical, fantastic events and powers of all kinds attributed to human beings—who sometimes become deities themselves.

There is also a gender complementarity difference between these groups of religions. Western faiths are based on a deity who is entirely masculine in character, associated mainly with the sky and cosmos, with a correspondingly pervasive effect on teachings and customs. Eastern faiths are both masculine and feminine in character, because God is perceived as having both masculine and feminine aspects (even though the social dimensions of these faiths are just as patriarchal as any society in the west). At the local level, the Eastern traditions also often have a strong indigenous element of connection to the Earth. So overall there is a complementarity between the Western element of transcendence, associating God with the sky and heaven, and the more feminine Eastern/indigenous identification of God with the Earth. The Earth is inseminated by rain from the sky, giving birth to plants that we eat, and which some animals eat before they are eaten. (And which decay back into the ground to become more plants. Such is the "circle of life.")

Finally, there is philosophical complementarity when it comes to God. Western traditions are monotheistic, and believe their God to be *personal*, having human characteristics. Eastern traditions are polytheistic, believing in *impersonal* Ultimate Realities of different kinds, the personal aspect getting embodied as those Ultimate Realities manifest themselves in their deity pantheons. Overall, Western religions appeal more to those aspects of our lives that are civilized, sensible, artificial and structured; Eastern religions to those which are naturalistic, connected, childlike and free.

The significance of this complementarity for mystical understanding is stated best in connection with the *yin* and the *yang* from Chinese thought. There is always some of the opposite in the other. In practical terms, what this means is that, while it is plainly impossible for all of us to "go back to nature," it is also impossible to set ourselves apart from it. The delusion that we can harmlessly alter the natural order is borne out when the laws of chemistry and physics inevitably produce the consequences, such as climate change and so on.

Abrahamic Religions—Common Dimensions

Judaism, Christianity and Islam identify with a single, transcendent God, moving beyond nature and the ordinary human condition. Since they wish to escape our normal condition, they go out of their way to contrast themselves with everyone else and are therefore traditionally *exclusivist*—each thinking that they are special in some way, the only true path to the Supreme Being.

It follows naturally from this that they are all *missionary* faiths, since good people naturally want to share their privileges with others who aren't yet as fortunate. Connected with this, they all have in their philosophies ideas about how they will one day dominate the world (this holds for Judaism as well, but in more subtle ways as we'll see).

By and large, the Western faiths regard humans as imperfect and inherently prone to sin, since orthodox doctrine reinforces the idea that we are fundamentally separate from God. As such, by and large they believe in *prophets*, not spiritual masters. Prophets are people chosen by God to deliver messages; as ordinary people they sometimes sin as well. Living spiritual masters from the East, on the other hand, are often thought by their followers to be sinless, although from a critical standpoint this is obviously far from true (Ch. 10).

Judaism

Judaism is unique in the way it is grounded in history, identifying itself as a people and ethnicity, as well as a religion—which renders it the most *confused* of all the religions in terms of being prone to dilemmas and paradoxes (see below). For these reasons, it is also the least mystical of the faiths overall, but the mysticism it does have is as great as any.

Though profoundly meaningful, the Jews' "chosen people" doctrine has been directly or indirectly responsible for most of the persecution they have endured down through the centuries. Aside from causing them to live in ritual purity apart from others (therefore offending them), and aside from constituting the philosophical foundation for most of its conflicts and disagreements with Christianity, this doctrine had economic consequences. Being a chosen people, after all the consequent persecution mentioned above, resulted in Jews being understood by the Catholic church, governments, etc. as a *sinful* people, which basically meant that they were the ones who ended up handling much of the money after currencies began being widely used in European countries. This is because money—which created a whole new level of temptation, since you can do anything if you have enough of it—was, and still is, tainted with sin. ("It's not about the money.") For a long time Christians weren't even supposed to touch it, so basically Jews, as a result also of papal pronouncements from the church and therefore from governments—ended up being the ones who did the *usury* (moneylending) to get economies going in medieval and early modern Europe. With the misunderstandings that naturally occur now and then in the course of business, Jews were the ones inexorably accused of wrongdoing since they were associated with greed and sin to begin with. This is one of the major reasons why various ruling powers either crushed or expelled Jews, again and again.

And that's not all. Our modern scientific understanding, of course, is that people are people and cultures are cultures—none of them is "chosen" by some external God. Traditionalist Jews (that is, those who haven't rejected or reinterpreted this idea), however, persist eternally in thinking and trying to confirm for themselves that they are. This famous *guilt dynamic* has resulted in more Nobel Prizes and awards among Jews than from any other ethnicity. Since we cannot all *be* Jews, their missionary activity is less direct: being role models for the rest of humanity, inspiring everyone else through exemplary conduct and achievement. It is in this sense that they would love to see everyone "become Jewish."

This uniquely secular dimension of Judaism is further reinforced by their custom of *arguing* with God, constantly reinterpreting the laws they were given by him at Mt Sinai. In the Old Testament, patriarchs like Abraham and Moses sometimes won arguments with God, and that tradition continues. Also, whereas there are traditions of philosophical debate in most of the other traditions, there *isn't* any philosophy—more abstract questions about God, etc.—in traditional Judaism. The whole religion (although some Jews don't think Judaism even is a religion) is focused around law and debating what it asks them to think and do in the world. As a Jew, you can *believe* anything you want about God/Self since there are no philosophical doctrines about what God is, including that he might not even exist, but you must *practice* (attend ceremony) to be a good Jew, and if you're really involved *argue* as well.

This ongoing scriptural reinterpretation reflects the changing circumstances of their history, which for Jews is very important; and again this reinforces the worldly orientation, motivating social and cultural interests that you really don't see in the other faiths, and outstanding involvements in politics and international affairs.

Because of all this, many Jews have particular difficulty achieving philosophical detachment from their cultural traditions, perpetrating conflict in the Middle East, primarily with Muslims who experience similar difficulties (see below). What should also be noted is that the founding fathers of the United States were to a large degree inspired by the Jews' "exodus" from the bondage of Egyptian slavery;[2] as a result, a sense of spiritual alliance with Israel has pervaded American political thought ever since.

Due to its ethnic aspect, finally, Judaism is more susceptible than other religions to *assimilation*—the loss of one's religion through immersion in general culture, especially as a result of intermarriage.

Christianity

Some scholars think that Christianity is the biggest religion because 1) of all the assistance it got from Constantine and the Roman Empire, but also 2) because it perhaps has the *most powerful myth* of all the religions—that of the baby Jesus. (This myth contributes important elements to Paschal Mystery dynamic mentioned on p. 126.) One prominent Christian apologist even said that Christianity is a *scientific* faith[3] insofar as it employs perhaps the most effective mechanism—"God became man so that man might become God," as both ancient and modern commentators have often put it.

Christianity has some interesting lesser-known contrasts with Judaism. In the latter faith, the traditional emphasis is on group obedience to law—to "do as God says," as it were. In Christianity, however, the emphasis is on imitating Christ—that is, to "be like God." The result is that all kinds of people become *saints* in Christianity, at least in its Catholic and Eastern Orthodox manifestations.

In Christianity and the Eastern faiths, therefore, it's possible for a human being in some sense to "become perfect," or to "reach perfection" through spiritual striving. Traditionally minded Jews, by contrast (along with similar Muslims), at least in principle don't believe in saints. All humans are fundamentally flawed; we get our teachings from prophets, whom God merely chooses to empower. For some Western conservatives, moreover, the faculty God possesses to empower and inspire normal flawed human beings to give teachings is something which he chooses to no longer do: all the great prophets lived in the past. We need only reinterpret their timeless teachings as time goes on. For others, however, this notion is part of the "golden age" fallacy. Saints and prophets exist today as much as they ever did (some would say a great deal more, due to mass spiritual evolution).

In the real world, educated and liberal-minded seekers in all these faiths usually overlook these differences, since again we all basically want the same things and approach our traditions with similar hopes and expectations. Most modern Jews have little interest in their debate traditions and are just as interested in deeper spirituality as anyone else. An enlightened teacher may be called a prophet if the prevailing belief is that nobody can be "perfect" or a saint if the belief is that you can. They teach effectively in either case, giving similar warnings against misconduct and similar encouragements regarding prayer and other basic practices.

It is not for nothing that Catholicism remains by far the largest branch of Christianity. This is not only because it preserves at least the idea of a living spiritual master (the Pope), but also because its followers can relate to God in a greater variety of ways: the Popes, the Madonna, the Patron saints, the Marian shrines and pilgrimage sites, or just through the majesty and trappings of all its ritual, ceremonies and architecture. This is why, in fact, some scholars think of Catholic Christianity as actually more polytheistic than monotheistic.

Christianity is also the religion with the greatest masculine prejudice. In Islam, at least, some of its prominent early followers were women, and there are traditions of women political leaders in some Muslim societies. In

Christianity however, not only were Jesus and all his disciples supposedly male (and the Catholic hierarchy ever since), but the celibacy on top of that, at least in practical terms, philosophically condemns the female body.

The Christian masculine leadership's fear of losing its position is not the prime motivator against too much feminine influence. Rather, it is fear of wrenching philosophical change at the core of the faith that would have to take place. Even in non-Catholic branches of the faith, too much feminine leadership would effectively decentralize, although not evict, Jesus as the core of the faith. Recall again the *yin* and the *yang*. Something which is 1% *yin* and 99% *yang* is going to be a very different animal than something that is 49% *yin* and 51% *yang*. Christianity would have to change too radically, perhaps even for most of the women who follow it.

Finally, an observation needs to be made here about Protestant Christianity, since it is philosophically unique in ways that motivate questionable behaviors among some of its adherents. This stems from their doctrine of the *priesthood of the believer*, which basically catapults the idea of one's individual relationship with God (which people in all religions have) above and beyond any authority, or any doctrine those authorities might espouse, no matter how basic or commonplace. If the idea of one's *unique relationship* with God is stressed enough, you end up seeing God through the lens of your own ideas and preferences.

Catholics must go through their priest and confessor. Jews and Muslims are subject to communal authority focusing around moral and legal codes. Hindus, Buddhists and Taoists all focus on the teachings of their sages, whether or not they're interested in full enlightenment. But the Protestant emphasis on the "the priesthood of the believer" is unique, and is the subconscious means by which some of its followers exempt themselves from moral and behavioral strictures which other religious leaders are more prone to obey.

Most Protestants are not affected in this way. They just prefer to practice Christianity without the elaborations of Catholicism. But some end up associating God with money, power, success, and sexual improprieties with some of their followers, as some scholars have long noted.

Islam

The most important, usually overlooked thing to understand about Islam is how the cultural circumstances of its origins profoundly affect it, even today. The relatively "uncivilized" character of its initial adherents impacted its teachings in a big way.

Both Christianity and Judaism grew up under or were shaped by political authority. In many ways, in its urban centers the Roman Empire did meet the criteria of what we would call a civil society—government, court system, schools, police, and so on. You may not have liked the laws, but you knew what they were, and if you had business with the authorities, reasonable manners, decorum and literacy were expected.

In ancient Arabia there was none of that. The region was inhabited by a shifting patchwork of nomadic tribes who fought and robbed each other periodically, had no allegiances outside their own group, and whose main virtue was an arrogant machismo. Muhammad had great difficulty civilizing some of his early followers; the necessity of accommodating fairly savage sensibilities is thought to be responsible for some of the problematic language in the Qur'an.

(In the religions where they occur, *revealed scriptures* are thought by traditional believers to be the word of God, period. The great majority of scholars, however, as well as some other followers of these faiths, understand such scriptures to reflect the background and conditionings of the human beings who produced them. An objective study of the religions must take this stance, not only to avoid privileging one faith over another, but in order to objectively study and evaluate historical data in the first place.)

Overall, the Qur'an is a marvelous document—contradicting itself like any good scripture does, and thereby having a strong mystical element. But there are negative and controversial passages, which, although historically understandable, are reason for concern. Some other major scriptures in the religions have such passages, but the Qur'an is the only major ancient one to devote significant space to discussing the other Abrahamic faiths, and not always in a complimentary way.

As a result of this, Islam has well-developed philosophical traditions of interpreting its major scripture in an almost completely metaphorical and allegorical way. What this means is that the actual literal meaning of some Qur'anic passages is all but completely irrelevant. Ideally in the faith, the book is meant to be *recited*, not read—unless one has the intellectual maturity to appreciate what most scholars think it really means to say. Inevitably however, literal-minded believers do read it and get it all wrong. This is the most profound reason for Islam's unfortunate association with terrorism.

The next least appreciated reason for this association is Islam's tradition of political dominance. This is also found in the other Abrahamic faiths, but neither Judaism nor Christianity was as historically successful as Islam was, partially because of the Muslim policy of toleration of other faiths throughout those times. Also, although Christianity dominated a huge area as well, it never had the tradition of a theocratic monarch (the Caliphate in Islam) ruling across entire states and nations. Some traditionalist Muslims remain attached to this ideal, and pursue it through insurgent activities.

In Christianity, the popes and Holy Roman emperors liked to think that they ruled "Christendom," but they were never more than merely influential. As time went on in the Middle Ages, the kings and queens of early Europe made major decisions more and more independently of these popes and emperors. And Jews, of course, were never more than a very small group of people, having only Israel to themselves in ancient times.

Another thing needing clarification, finally, is the contribution of Sharia Law to the anxiety surrounding Islam. The Muslim legal system is, of course, responsible for the faith's various controversial customs; but there's more to it than that. Precisely because it has a *legal system*, Islam is construed as being threatening to a host country's existing "way of life" in a way that another religion would not be.

If it weren't so small (14.5 million followers), this would be true of Judaism as well. In contrast to Christianity, both Islam and Judaism are communal faiths, in that everyone must submit to the laws given them by their respective prophets. To reiterate (see above in the Christianity section), these faiths "do as God says." If Judaism were the big religion, the Torah's *Halakah* literature would be making people nervous, not Sharia Law.

More obvious contributors to Islam's association with terrorism include the various diplomatic and historical affairs in the Middle East over the course of the 20th century.

Notes

Introduction

1   Readers familiar with critical theory should realize that I will be trying to define some things which are beyond definition. True—religion doesn't exist outside of culture. But that's not our main topic.

Chapter 1

1   Collected Works, p. 509.

2   Wayne Dyer has some of the best material on manifestation. See his *Wishes Fulfilled: Mastering the Art of Manifestation*.

3   Google "Quantum mechanisms for paranormal phenomena," and you'll see what I mean.

4   Deepak Chopra and Amrit Goswami are two authors who explain this in more detail. For more conservative classics in the field, see Fritof Capra's *The Tao of Physics* and Gary Zukav's *Dancing Wu-li Masters.*

5   At any point in history there is an apocalyptic minority declaring that a new age or the end of the world is around the corner. What is unique about the current era of history isn't excessive warfare, cruelty, starvation, corruption, and so on—if you look at planet-wide, per capita data, many of those indices have actually improved. It's the environmental crisis. Unless many things about our behavior change soon, there is good reason to think that much of human civilization is in real jeopardy. Awareness of this crisis, and the suffering we're bringing on ourselves connected with it, seem to have been prerequisite for the planetary awakening that many believe is now taking place. What this means for mystical awareness is that it will no longer be confined to the small number of people traditionally associated with it.

Chapter 2

1   A concept first articulated by German anthropologist Rudolph Bastian.

2   C.G. Jung's signature contribution to human self-understanding. No psychologist has had a greater influence on popular mystical spirituality.

3 This is Sigmund Freud's patriarchal theory of atheism—perhaps the best such theory out there. For more, see his book *Future of an Illusion*.

4 Basically, the idea that the simplest solution to a problem is the best. For some people, God doesn't have to exist because the laws of nature account for everything.

5 The construct of "maturity" is not clearly defined in psychology, probably to avoid elitism as much as from difficulty in defining indices by which it might be measured. In this book, maturity is defined according to the opinion of most educated persons who admire virtues such as thoughtfulness, conscientious and hard work, good self-care, and dedication to causes and issues which enhance the well-being of people and other life forms on the planet.

6 If God is unknowable, incomprehensible, and so on, and physical reality is knowable, then we can think of the supernatural as encompassing the realm in between. The "mechanical" things discussed in chapters 7, 9, 10, and 11 all occur within that realm.

7 When it comes to metaphysics, circularity doesn't so much imply that an argument is bad; instead, it serves to demonstrate the impossibility of intellectually understanding some profound things.

8 This term is not used in academic psychology. To acknowledge the subconscious would imply that a difference exists between it and the unconscious, which is the preferred term. The former would be specific to the individual's measurable sensory experience in this life; the latter therefore would have to embrace realms of knowledge and experience for which there is no empirical evidence, such as universal archetypes and experiences from previous lifetimes.

Chapter 3

1 To some of the Buddha's modern students, it only seems that way since he deemphasized its importance so much. In the *Udana*, a volume from the Pali Canon, he does explicitly tell his early followers that there exists something very profound and invisible to the senses, which he called *Nirvana*. (Later on this concept was projected onto the universe as the *Dharmakaya Buddha*, which is basically equivalent to the Hindu *Atman/Brahman*. For some groups the former term was personalized as a single, primary deity—Amithaba Buddha. Thus, for many Buddhists, an external monotheistic deity becomes part of basic doctrine, for the most part completely contradicting Siddhartha Gautama's original teaching.)

2 If you've studied Christianity, you may associate *mystics* with historical saints and luminaries who may have spoken of their religion as being the only way. That is because they either didn't know that other religions existed or, more commonly perhaps, never got enough the exposure necessary to appreciate them as full-fledged religions like their own. Enlightened beings do not automatically know everything (Ch.12,S.2C).

3   For a good example, see the documentary *Unmistaken Child*, about the search, discovery and installation of a new reincarnated Tibetan Buddhist lama.

4   As you grow up, you might construct for yourself a "better" ego, but it's still an ego. As Bart Marshall put it, "You can't polish a turd; it won't take a shine." (Personal remarks, Philadelphia, PA Sept. 2011)

5   My own condensed summary of Erik Erikson's criteria.

6   See John Welwood's *Towards a Psychology of Awakening* for more on this.

7   Richard Fowler's *Stages of Faith* is good for understanding transitions between stages of spirituality. He takes as his starting points the works of Erikson, Kohlberg, and other 20th century developmental theorists.

8   Eckhart Tolle is the classic modern example. He recounts his background and awakening experience in his book *The Power of Now*.

9   I don't mention names for reasons explained in Ch. 12 (Int.) But if you google phrases like "Who's awake?" or "Self-Inquiry for Enlightenment" and use your discrimination, you'll find all kinds of people.

10 A tendency especially among Buddhist-oriented seekers is to dismiss such questions, because you can never know for sure anyway and they might distract you from your practice. There is often an element of pride in this, amounting to a rejection of *all* beliefs for the sake of going one's own way. More reasonable attitudes accept that it is necessary, at some point, to take important questions seriously and respond to them in a meaningful way.

Chapter 4

1   This is from the *Ethics* (Pt.1,Pr.17,Sch.).

2   I should say here that, in their emotional moments, even intelligent followers of gurus in devotionally oriented Hindu groups will refer to their teacher as God, although also realizing that the guru is "just" a human being.

3   Although for complex reasons Islam has a poor reputation overall for women's issues, one of Muhammad's signature contributions to world ethics was a conscious platform for more equitable treatment of women, granting them rights in marriage, divorce, inheritance, property ownership and other basic privileges as citizens in their society. The oppressive customs we hear about basically predate Islam, but became strongly associated with the faith over time.

Chapter 5

1 See Ch.2,N.1.

2 The best material on archetypes I think is from Jung himself, in his *Analytical Psychology: Its Theory and Practice.*

3 The idea that the mind itself determines the structure of reality has always been a basic premise of Hindu and Buddhist metaphysics. As far as I know, it didn't start gaining ground in Western academic circles until George Berkeley came out with his "immaterialism" philosophy in the early 18th Century.

4 See Fowler—especially his explanation of what he calls the *Mythic-Literal* stage of faith.

5 A paraphrase from Joseph Campbell's *The Inner Reaches of Outer Space.* The theory of universal archetypes—the idea that certain profound ideas are shared by all humanity in our collective unconscious—while taken for granted by most all mystically inclined seekers, is not subscribed to by many anthropologists who study folklore. The latter's view is usually more "culture-specific," understanding the functions of a society's myths on the empirical level.

6 This well-known observation from C.G. Jung is important for how it links spirituality to the social sciences.

Chapter 6

1 In broad outline, scholars will recognize elements of the "common sense" evolutionary theory of religion first developed by the 19th century anthropologist Edward Tylor. Although this theory has long been discredited as *strictly* true since there are exceptions to it, as far as I'm concerned it retains a good deal of *general* truth, especially as a series of insights valuable for its explanation of why certain forms of religion are dominant.

2 This stemmed from a number of mostly English philosophers in the 17th and 18th centuries, who were impressed by the laws of classical physics elucidated by Galileo, Newton, and others. These writers basically took one step further Thomas Aquinas' classic Argument from Design (for God's existence) found in his *Summa Theologica.* I include Scientific Deism in my list of paradigms because rational and scientific ways of thinking are more prevalent than ever before.

3 The late 20th century astronomer Carl Sagan was certainly one of the greatest "scientific romanticists"—he obviously considered the idea of God superfluous because, for him, the awe, wonder, passion and so forth connected with science *was* God, although he wouldn't have called it that.

4 This is from Thomas Merton's *New Seeds of Contemplation*.

5 See Freud (Ch.2,N.3). Such material can be valuable in helping some believers see through commonly held, superficial ideas about God.

6 Fowler (Ch.3,N.7) has a great concept in his book called the *Shared Center of Value and Power* (SCVP). It's not a worldview, but is worth mentioning because it pinpoints perhaps the greatest ultimate concern that most people have, at least with regard to immediate, meaningful experience. The SCVP is the mythos, or connection of stories, which families develop as the generations pass and events occur. It is celebrated most powerfully on holidays when everyone is gathered around, perhaps with some drinks, and reiterates stories about what so-and-so did when they got drunk that time back in college, and the like. It is a more localized version of what indigenous peoples and the religions do when reenacting their most important myths. The Christian passion play is a well-known example of the latter. As I understand them, SCVPs and reenactments are primarily about reaffirming identity. The mystical orientation, on the other hand, is universal and no longer concerned with family and ethnicity. It *has* no identity.

7 This concept plays a huge part in Spinoza's philosophy, and rightly so. In many cases we form degrees of attachment to whatever we associate ourselves with. It may take a person decades of therapeutic work to *dissociate* himself (his own self-concept) from, for example, the sexual abuse he experienced, so that he is no longer tormented by feelings and memories around it, but it can be done. The British philosopher David Hume—in all likelihood without realizing it—implied astonishing and accurate things back in the 18th century about enlightenment when he pointed out in his *Enquiry Concerning Human Understanding* that our entire sense of day-to-day continuity (such as, thinking that the sun will rise the next morning) comes ultimately from such associations—which need not necessarily be made. Enlightened beings make no such assumptions, even though they're familiar with them.

8 The title of a (not very readable) book by the mid-20th century religion scholar Frithjof Schuon.

9 Should you think that none of these corresponds to your view of reality at all, then I invite you to examine your attitude. It's very common today to have a prideful, cynical inner disposition to the effect that nobody can tell you anything. But how *does* the universe work? Are you refusing to really *encounter* that question? It's certainly fine to go your own way. You can, for example, be an *anarchist* if you want (although that's primarily a political philosophy), but if you're interested in spiritual growth, sooner or later you will be giving up such views of the world.

Chapter 7

1   Deepak Chopra's *Life After Death* is very good.

2   The "hungry ghosts" of folk Chinese religion (mostly Buddhist and Taoist) are a good example.

3   The famous heavenly hierarchy of Chinese Religion is probably the best known example of this (and certainly came about due to Confucian influence).

4   Full enlightenment certainly occurs in these traditions, even if there isn't a lot of philosophy in their oral traditions explaining it.

5   The Catholic *purgatory* is the best-known example.

6   The idea of levels of heaven and hell is most classically illustrated in Dante's *Divine Comedy* (pub. 14th century). Due to its stature in world literature, it would almost be true to say that the Church adopted the *Comedy* as a kind of default description of the afterlife, for anyone who was curious about it.

7   Spinoza develops this idea somewhere in the *Ethics*.

8   There are numerous examples of this. In his *Ascent of Mt. Carmel*, for example (Book II), St. John of the Cross in Christianity writes of the seeking soul at one point: "Indeed, it is God by participation."

9   Because they are either outright or relatively non-theistic, Buddhist and Taoist philosophy don't describe the workings of God as an organized, creative entity. You have to go to sophisticated Hindu-related systems for the best systematic material. Of these, the *Trika* or Kashmir Shavism system I think is exceptional. Modern translations of classic works and commentaries on them from that school of thought, such as the *Spanda Karikas* and *Vijnana Bhairava* (Motilal Banarsidass, Mumbai, India) should be consulted. In recent years, some of these have been published by SUNY Press, New York.

10   One good book that casts modern physics as a kind of scientific theology, while drawing similarities and insights from the religions, is Fred Alan Wolfs' *The Spiritual Universe*.

11   I believe this expression is from the British philosopher Alfred North Whitehead.

12   Again, Eckhart Tolle is the best example. See Ch. 3,N.4.

Chapter 8

1   Philosophically, grace and self-effort comprise a chicken-and-egg issue: as God's signature creatures, we already have grace; but paradoxically we need to exert ourselves to find more of it.

2 In the East, indirect references to this term go all the way back to the *Rig Veda*, a few of whose verses inspired the well known Sanskrit *neti, neti* (not this, not this) concept of Advaita Vedanta Hindu philosophy. In modern times, self-inquiry is perhaps most associated with the teachings of the 20th century Indian sages Ramana Maharishi ("Who am I?") and Nisargadatta Maharaj. Its most classic references in the West date first to Plato's Socratic dialogues, and later to the development of the *via negativa* (negative way) and apophatic theology in Christian mysticism.

3 Tai chi seems to have evolved out of Chinese martial arts traditions for more spiritual purposes; chi gong was always meant to cultivate spiritual energy as part of mystical Taoism, and later, Buddhism.

4 I should mention in this connection that researchers in modern physics frequently deal with equally profound issues, which are often merely more "concrete" ways of exploring the same questions that the scriptures do. For example, philosophically the enlightened state is said to be the experience of neither being (existence) nor nonbeing (nonexistence). The observer effect in physics involves this question. When scientists study either the very big (the edge of the universe) or the very small (subatomic particles), at a certain point, the limitations of the very medium through which the phenomenon is being perceived (light) through the instruments involved causes the observer to inevitably create or imagine something, instead of definitely seeing something.

5 For those interested, the 11th Century classic Jewish thinker Maimonides (known to scholars as Raumbaum) details 12 different "levels of giving" in his *Guide to the Perplexed*.

6 This phrase is from Thomas Merton's *New Seeds of Contemplation*.

7 See Ch.3,N.4.

8 As a pursuit, this refers to becoming more and more conscious *that* you're dreaming while you're dreaming. To some degree, this happens to everyone as their spiritual journey proceeds, whether or not they take a particular interest in it.

9 One reference is Shaun Nevins' *The Celibate Seeker: An Exploration of Celibacy as a Modern Spiritual Practice*, TAT Foundation Press.

10 See Junpo Denis Kelly Roshi, *The Heart of Zen: What it Really Takes for Spiritual Enlightenment*.

11 I should mention that a significant number of highly respected, modern teaching influences (the Pathwork, Conversations with God, Course in Miracles, among others) were all "channeled" in some sense—either by mediums in the classic mold who, to whatever extent, did turn their bodies and minds over to a source entity, or by writers who claim to have received their teachings by listening to and transcribing material from inner voices without going into a deep trance. Needless to say, aside from the writers' sincerity and that of their close associates, there is no way to ascertain that the material did originate from disembodied entities and not from the writers' own minds.

12 Robert Bly's *Iron John* and Sam Keen's *Fire in the Belly* are good contemporary references involving this topic.

13 Anthropologists call this *liminality*, an "in-between" state of ambiguity and disorientation.

14 Near-death experiences, usually on the operating table.

15 Extra Sensory Perception. In the early and mid-20th century, a fair amount of research was conducted on ESP and related psychic phenomena. Interest in such research today has faded for a number of reasons. The mainstream scientific community has mostly concluded that such powers have never been satisfactorily demonstrated within rigorous laboratory conditions. Other people, including some scientists, take such phenomena for granted from their own or others' experience, and recognize from spiritual teachings that, by their very nature, such phenomena do not conform to structured conditions or rules. Finally, for some people, current research in modern physics is slowly substantiating the true bases in subtle reality for these phenomena (Ch.1,N.3).

16 Chapter 4 of Patanjali's *Yoga Sutras* from Hinduism is the best known. For some scholars, the only thing that makes these sorts of powers believable it the fact that accounts of them occur in the literature of almost all the world's mystical traditions.

17 This amounts to a more subtle version of Nietzsche's *Ubermensch* or "Superman," which so captivated Nazi Germany and provided an underlying, philosophical motivation for Hitler's attempt to create a Third Reich through World War II. In that case, excessive pride resulted in an ideal warrior role model of superior strength and power. Today, equally proud Dr. Frankensteins seek to have us know and control everything in a way Nietzsche could never have imagined.

18 My personal impression of the teacher—but some of them (or their organizations) are particularly sensitive about being quoted.

Chapter 9

1 This is from his transcribed volume *I am That*—one of the most valuable books ever published by an Eastern sage in the Western Hemisphere.

2 Most Hindu-related teachers use this metaphor. In terms of seminal Western references, we perhaps know it best from Freud's "oceanic experience" speculation about an infant's awareness in the womb.

3 Paul Hedderman, personal remarks, Philadelphia 2013.

4 I should mention that Sanskrit terms (*chakra, nadi,* etc.) tend to be the ones used by all groups who deal with these phenomena, since the whole yoga system connected with Hinduism was the first truly mystical regimen of practices to become widely known in the west.

5 There is controversy over how much the Hindu system—being the oldest and most developed—may have influenced the others, but in general the other systems do seem to have developed independently. I prefer to think of it this way, since it's not helpful to privilege one major cultural/historical paradigm over another.

6 For example, the *Prataybinjnahrydyam* (Motilal Banarsidass), another document associated with the Kashmir Shavism system in India, states this directly.

7 Any health condition has as spiritual and cognitive component as well as a physical component. The greater the former, the more a good alternative healer can help; that's why his or her state of consciousness is important. Within that, the specific *gift* the person has predisposes the healer to work with a certain established modality or combination of modalities, or sometimes to invent his or her own.

8 Allopathic medicine acknowledges *psychosomatic* influences on certain conditions, but would stop short of asserting that belief by itself has such as strong influence on the presence or severity of a condition.

9 Huston Smith may have been the first one to coin this term, at least in the Hinduism section of his video series *The World's Religions.*

Chapter 10

1 Joseph Campbell's well known expression.

2 Just like people who are dying sometimes do, as Elizabeth Kubler-Ross elucidated for us years ago.

3 The reincarnation scenario is no exception to this. We don't remember previous lives (except at advanced stages of practice, apparently), so people have to pick up where they left off with new awakenings.

4 Eckhart Tolle, personal remarks, Omega Institute, July 2013.

5 In another context (Irish Catholic), Jeanette Winterson's book *Why Be Happy When You Could Be Normal?* details similar religiously motivated generational misery. The title is actually a question that Simmons' mother asked her at one point!

6 Maharaj, N., P. 74.

7 Eckhart Tolle (Ch.3.,N.8) is probably the best known example of this. As he recounts in the introduction to his book *The Power of Now,* he was a philosophy student who awoke all at once, at least partially as a result of suicidal depression, and didn't know what had happened to him until he studied spiritual texts afterwards.

8 A teacher I respect told me this, and it sounds plausible enough. Internally, a lot can happen in the 4 or 5 seconds it takes to fall the 300-odd feet from that bridge, and then to smash into San Francisco Bay!

9 This is not uncommon among modern-day devotees of Eastern traditions, especially those who follow living teachers. The evidence for this may never be more than anecdotal; but it is there and you can only get a sense of it by "asking around" widely enough. Historical examples include the Indian poet-saint Tukaram (16th Cent.), and the 6th century founder of religious Taoism, Chang Dao-Ling.

10 Again, Eckhart Tolle is perhaps the best-known example. As he recounts in the *The Power of Now*, he made the breakthrough while under severe psychological stress, and only figured out what had happened to him later through his own research.

11 In some groups, most notably Islam, the "institution" can be represented merely by a couple of already initiated people looking on.

12 This word has a meaning independent of Christianity: an attitude or understanding that is all-embracing or accepting.

13 Another way of putting this is that such exclusivist views necessarily exclude any understanding of how non-believers as well as believers can emerge from the same God/Self, at the most basic level of creation.

14 One place to see this in action is Edna Hartley's film about Balinese and Indonesian religion, in her collection *Meditation, Prayer and Trance*.

Chapter 11

1 I coined this term for myself after reading Spinoza, as I'm sure others have done the same from their own sources.

2 This refers to Eastern masters, since their more naturalistic philosophy encompasses the body and all its processes. You'd never hear this kind of thing from traditionally minded Abrahamic clergy.

3 Jeremy Taylor says pretty much the same thing on p. 32 of his book *Dream Work*. Of course, to the external observer watching you sleep, nothing has happened, but according to the metaphysics being discussed here, the dreamer does actually go halfway back to his or her maker, and therefore temporarily "dissolves" halfway. This is one of the paradoxes of reality that is somehow "perceived and understood" in the enlightened state.

4 This is the most basic outline of the monistic scheme of creation. Hindu, Buddhist and Taoist philosophies portray it in greater detail.

5   A comprehensive way of understanding Jung's collective unconscious. In this context, I might clarify the power and universality of the serpent as a spiritual symbol, since there are three pictures of them in the book. Snakes are 1) sinuous and often unnoticed, like the deep, hidden desires and issues in our minds; 2) often dangerous when they bite, causing transformative processes to occur in our bodies, symbolic of healing (the fact that in reality that process goes in the other direction—toward death—is unimportant, since both involve transformation); 3) bright and new-looking after shedding their skin, symbolic of cleansing, a new start, initiation, and 4) subtle in their movements and expressionless, suggesting detachment, wisdom and perspective.

6   In Eastern thought, the sixth sense is said to be the mind. It perceives things about reality that the other senses do not, as a result of thought. An argument can also be made that it intuits things directly without processing the sensations it receives, just like the other senses, even if we do not know exactly what the sensations are that the mind receives in order to accomplish this intuition. Clearly, any communication technology working on that level would have to utilize mechanisms currently unknown to science.

7   The late Master Sumbramunyia Swami of the Saiva Siddhantha Church wrote a book entitled *Affirmations*, which has a good one: *I can, I will, I am able.*

8   *Ibid.*

9   Victor Frankl used this phrase in one of his books… for the life of me I cannot remember which.

Chapter 12

1   This commonly happened (and still happens) to Americans who went to visit Hindu- and Buddhist-related groups when the greatest wave of teachers from these faiths came to this country in the latter part of the 20th century, just as it happens now to some of us who visit the ever more common Islamic places of worship (mosques) which are springing up around the country. Historical and sociological explanations cannot touch this. The fact that many of us were and are disaffected from our Judeo-Christian backgrounds for complex reasons does not account for the lifelong extraordinary depth and affinity that someone may mysteriously feel for a tradition that was completely alien to him or her, up until that point.

2   As mentioned in Ch.10, note 9, it is a common experience among followers of living masters to receive inner messages through dreams, hunches or intuitions that the person attributes to the master's influence. Again, if you lack any experience of this, you can really only get a sense of it by speaking to devotees and delving into the anecdotal literature written by them. The content of such messages directs seekers into new activities that teach them more about themselves—and not always comfortably. Because the teacher is not longer actually alive, and therefore not longer manifests an aura (C.11,S.4) which is as powerful, it is likely that this does not occur as often among followers of deceased luminaries such as Christ, Muhammad and Abraham. (In the words of Bubba Free John, a teacher from the 1970's and 80's, "Dead gurus can't kick ass.")

3   Examples would be Guru Har Kishen of the Sikh lineage in 17th century India, Shri Chinmoy in late 20th century America and Europe, and of course the Dalai Lamas and other such lineages within Tibetan Buddhism. The fact that enlightenment does sometimes occur among young people, and also that infants are undoubtedly born in a state of precognitive innocence at least similar to enlightenment, hints at the possibility that some rare individuals retain the enlightened state since birth. This is popularly believed to be the case with a number of Eastern saints, past and present.

4   Interested readers can research this easily enough. Aside from what was said earlier about celibacy (Ch.8,S.16) and unethical behavior (Ch.9,S.2&3), it is interesting to speculate regarding underlying causes. Do the spiritual energies such teachers channel cause subtle forms of dementia to occur over time, resulting in compromised moral integrity?

5   It's little wonder that this term ended up getting used for the popular movie series. Extraterrestrials—who in the *Avatar* movies are us—incarnate themselves on other worlds, although with imperialist rather than spiritual objectives.

Appendix 2

1   The idea that a mantra protects the person who uses it is a general philosophical observation which has long been made by spiritual teachers. For just one example, see the website of the Spiritual Research Foundation. If you ask around Hindu-related group especially, many people will be able to give you accounts of this.

Appendix 3

1   Although largely discredited by most mainstream academics (due, at least in part, to their culture-specific perspectives), this concept from the French thinker Jean Jacques Rousseau in the 18th century obviously has some truth to it.

2   This event is thought by most mainstream biblical historians and archeologists—even Jewish ones—to be largely if not entirely mythical.

3   This is found in C.S. Lewis' *Mere Christianity*.

General Bibliography

In contrast to the rest of this book, in which I have endeavored to be objective, the list below does, finally, reflect "my own experience"—at least of powerful and helpful reading. If I have written anything of value, these works have helped me do so, although mostly in an indirect and underlying way. A few I basically disagree with, but they were instructive concerning important views held by many others.

Dass, R. *Journey of Awakening: A Meditator's Guidebook.* New York:Bantam Books, 1978.

Dass, R. *Be Here Now.* San Cristobal, NM: Lama Foundation, 1971.

Durant, W. *The Story of Philosophy.* New York: Simon and Schuster,1926.

Frankl, V. *Man's Search for Meaning: An Introduction to Logotherapy.*New York: Simon and Schuster, 1959.

Fromm, E. *The Art of Loving.* New York: Harper and Row, 1956.

John, St. *Ascent of Mt. Carmel.* Washington, DC: Institute of CarmeliteStudies, 1979. (Written in late 16th Cent. Spain.)

Jung, C. *Two essays in Analytical Psychology.* Princeton, NJ: PrincetonUniversity Press, 1966.

Kelly Roshi, D. *Mondo Zen: Ego Deconstruction Koans.* HollowBones/Friends of Zen, 2009.

Keen, S. *Hymns to an Unknown God: Awakening the Spirit in EverydayLife.* New York: Bantam, 1994.

Leshan, L. *How to Meditate: A Guide to Self-Discovery.* Boston, MA: Little,Brown & Company, 1974.

Lewis, C.S. *Mere Christianity.* New York: HarperCollins, 1952.

M., Nisargadatta, *I am That.* Durham, NC: Acorn Press, 1984.

Merton, T. *New Seeds of Contemplation.* New York: New Directions,1972.

Muktananda, S. *Play of Consciousness.* San Francisco: Harper and Row,1978.

Novak, M., & J. *Tell Me Why: a father Answers his Daughter's QuestionsAbout God.* New York: Pocket Books, 1998.

Prabhavananda, S. & Isherwood, C. *Bhagavad Gita.* Hollywood, CA:Vedanta Press, 1944.

Rahula, W. *What the Buddha Taught*. New York: Grove/Atlantic, 1974.

Singh, J. (trans.) *Shiva Sutras: the Yoga of Supreme Identity*. Delhi: MotilalBanarsidass, 1979. (Probably written in 9th century India.)

Spinoza, B. *The Ethics Geometrically Demonstrated*, translated by Samuel Shirley, Hackett Publishing, Ind. 1982 (other existing translationsare impossibly boring to read).

Subramanian, K. (ed.) *The Mahabharata*, Bharatyia Vidya Bhavan,Mumbai, India 2014.

Subramunyiaswami, M. *The Self God, The Power of Affirmation* and othershort works. San Francisco: Comstock House, 1973.

Tweedie, I. *Daughter of Fire*. Nevada City: Blue Dolphin Publishing, 1979.

Tolle, E. *The Power of Now*. Vancover, BC: Namaste Publishing, 1997.

Watts, A. *The Book: on the Taboo Against Knowing Who You Are*. NewYork: Vintage Books, 1972.

Wilmer, H. *Practical Jung: Nuts and Bolts of Jungian Psychology*, ChironPublications, Wilamette, IL, 1987.

Zukav, G. *The Dancing Wu Li Masters: an Overview of the New Physics.*New York: William Morrow, 1979.

Acknowledgments

It is difficult to sum up all my important influences, especially since so many of them are spiritual teachers and writers of various kinds. Those I will not list for reasons mentioned in the book. But my life has also been positively impacted by many people in more worldly positions, as well as by able helpers in different capacities, some of them deceased. They include all my college instructors in graduate school; all the therapists of various kinds who have helped me in one way or another; the entire current and former Siddha Yoga Sangam of Philadelphia and beyond with whom I am or was acquainted; all the great *kirtan* musicians who perform at the Omega Institute in Rhinebeck, New York; all my friends and acquaintances connected with Hollow Bones Zen, the Mankind Project, the TAT Foundation and of course my wife, Marsha, for her love, encouragement and impeccable editing (when I chose to go along with it).

And special thanks also to Juliet, whose portraits I thought were better than those of five professional artists, even though she is still in school as of this writing!

CPSIA information can be obtained at www.ICGtesting.com
Printed in the USA
BVOW05s2251290216

438562BV00005B/8/P